Stronger
Every Day

Tracie Hunsberger

ISBN-13:9781974173150

ISBN-10:1974173151

DEDICATION

To my husband, children and grandchildren: You are each a gift from God and have brought a great fulfillment to my life. I love you forever and always.

To the Bennett family, Stefani, Andy and Shelby: Thank you for sharing Bailey with us. His smile, strength and laughter have forever impacted my heart. During the times when I didn't have the strength to carry on, I would see Bailey in my news feed pounding away at those push-ups. I knew that if he could go through his journey with a smile, I could too.

Bailey Bennett June 5, 2006 - June 7, 2016

To our Heavenly Father, The Lord Jesus Christ and The Holy Spirit: Thank You for saving us and for allowing us to share this message with Your children. May You receive all the glory!

CONTENTS

ACKNOWLEDGMENTS

To my friend and editor Laura Ritchie: Thank you for standing with me. I couldn't have asked for a more loyal and supportive friend. Thank you for partnering with me to reach out to the world with a message of God's love and faithfulness.

CHAPTER 1

THE INTRODUCTION

Tracie Hunsberger

Stronger

Every Day

Hard-won truths of a life lived by an author unafraid to face the battle with God at her side.

I got a call asking me to start writing my story. It was not a huge surprise because it had happened before. The timing was never right, but this time it was different. When I picked up the phone and began talking, something in my spirit jumped. It was as though God was telling me, "Tracie, I know you have been through a lot, and I need you to let Me use your story. There are hurting people that need to hear your story. They need to know that I am always there with them even in the midst of the chaos."

At some point in our lives we all have to uncover what our purpose is. Mine is to bring the Gospel to a hurting world and to show that God has always been in the background fighting for all of us.

In my life, I have always been very transparent. Some will likely wonder why I decided to open myself up like this. I share not only my story of abuse but also my weaknesses that became evident along the way. Darkness hates light. Darkness has tried to prevent me from living the way I was born to live, happy and healthy. BUT GOD! God always stepped in and brought light. Now He is asking me to take a spotlight and shine it on myself.

When we shine light, darkness has to flee. But, this is not only for me. It is for all of us!

John 1:5 (NIV) The light shines in the darkness, and the darkness cannot overcome it.

This is not only my story, it is all our stories. It is for the underdogs of the world...the ones that keep hearing the dark voices that tell us we are broken. The voices that remind us that we are not going to make it. "If only I had been born into a better family, then the world would not be so cruel." Satan torments us all with feelings of inadequacies. We see flashbacks in our minds....memories that remind us that our past would like to disqualify us from our future.

This book is for every child that hears they will never escape because there is no way out. They believe that they are deserving of the way the world is treating them. It is for every person who shuts out memories of abuse to survive. It is for those who have battle wounds from cancer or from watching a loved one fight a battle for themselves. It is for those fighting to keep their marriage alive despite being two broken people.

This is our story. God has given our hurt a voice.

He is replying, "I am sorry that you hurt. This was never My plan. Come close to Me, and I will heal your broken pieces. I will pick you up when you can't get up on your own. I will show you the plan I have for you and I will help you get stronger every day!"

Walk with me through my journey. You will find the strength and the healing that God brought you here to find. Perhaps you will find hidden in the pages of this book your own story. A word may jump off the page reminding you of someone you love. This story may give you a glimpse into a world you have never seen by opening your eyes to the hurts of others.

You may find in these pages the pieces of you that are still broken.

Above all, I pray that you find God's love story for you. He held the hand of His daughter walking her through the valleys then delivering her to the other side. Through His amazing and powerful love, He restores the cracks inside each of us. You will finally declare that God is able to turn your travesty into your triumph. At the end of this book, may you never let an obstacle stand in the path of all that God has for you. With God, all things are possible!

Chapter 1 Application: Today open yourself up to the possibilities. Give yourself permission to dream again. Allow your mind to pick up the dreams that you set on the shelf afraid that they would never come to a reality in your life. Listen to the voice of God calling to you. He wants to take you on a journey. Will you trust Him to bring you safely to the other side?

Prayer: Heavenly Father, I thank you for every person who has and will come across this book. I thank you that you watch over them, protect them, lead them and guide them, and give them peace. Bring them into the fullness of everything You have started in them. Thank You that You enlighten the eyes of their understanding so that they may know the hope to which You have called them. I pray that they come into a revelation of the depth of Your love for them. I thank You that no weapon formed against them will prosper, that every tongue that rises against them will be silenced, and that their vindication will come from You. Ephesians 1:18 - Ephesians 3:18 - Isaiah 54:17.

CHAPTER 2

A ROUGH START

My name is Tracie Lynn Hunsberger (Beck). My husband Eric and I serve faithfully in the ministry working beside each other every step of the way. We founded Romans 831 Ministries where we travel with the Gospel of Jesus. God has called us to let people know that God is passionately in love with each and every one of us. He never gives up on us. He sets people free and restores to them everything that the enemy has stolen. As sell outs to Him, we will go anywhere He sends us. We will never tell Him no.

I am the baby in my family. At forty-two years old, my hair is showing a few gray strands. My blonde hair is bunched into a my ponytail as I sit in a cozy shirt and blue jeans curled up with laptop writing this. Covering me is a blanket and my black mini-schnauzer, Willow, curled up next to me.

I am in a great place, but that has not always been the case. I fill myself up with God's Word. I spend time with Him in prayer. As I do, I become more unwavering and continue to get stronger every day.

My oldest sister is Julie. She is the responsible one...someone had to be. She is a banker at Chase Bank in our hometown. At the age of 16, she married Greg. They have two children. Recently, Greg was diagnosed with small cell lymphoma and is going through chemotherapy. This month he received the words that everyone on a journey with cancer longs to hear. REMISSION! Julie's eyes are bright and beautiful...sometimes, I think I can see through to her soul. She has always been the mother figure in my life. As both "mother" and sister, I enjoy the two roles she fills for me. I love our time together. I have watched her 5' 7" frame become frail and thin as time passes. Bearing the responsibility of caring for all her siblings, has been a full-time job. We were a handful, and she carries the worries of what could happen to us in her heart.

Next in line is Patricia. We call her Patty. She is the tallest of the siblings at 5' 9". She gets her height from our grandfather. She is not as talkative as the rest of us. Birth order likely played a role. She did not have the competition that I did. She served in the Army Reserves then as a janitor in our local school system until she became too sick to work. In 1974 when she was a baby, she lost oxygen when we had a house fire. Patty now lives with COPD, a lung disease. She and her husband Allen have raised two daughters together. Patty brings an inviting presence into any room. It's hard not to feel anything but love in her presence. My kids call her "Whopper Patty" because she always brings them chocolate malt balls when she visits.

Third in line is my sister Barbara. We call her Barbie like the doll. Barbie also served in the Army Reserves and currently works in the local school cafeteria. She likely brightens every person's day in her path. Her name comes from our mom. She cares deeply. I don't think I have ever seen her angry. She has extreme protective instincts for her siblings. Watch out though...if there is a baby in the room, she will steal it, feed it fudge and will ignore the "mom look" that we all know so well. Barbie is also 5' 7" with blonde hair and a thin frame. She and her husband Jay have raised three children.

My next sister is Kimberly. We call her Kim or sometimes we call her by her middle name, Bernice. It irritates her and makes us smile. While in the Air Force, she was deployed to Afghanistan. She married Bryan, her high school sweetheart, and together they raised three children. Kim works for Slice Plus Technologies as the Chief Financial Officer. She stands about 5' 5" tall with shoulder length blonde hair. She serves in her church and also volunteers for community outreaches. Kim and Bryan take in children through Safe Families. When parents are unable to care for their children during periods of transition or medical treatments, they provide temporary supervision. Kim rushes to our aid anytime we need her...even if we don't even know that we do. She just knows.

My next sibling is Robert Allen Beck, Junior. We called him Bobby. The abuse Bobby endured from our father was severe. When dad looked at him, there was hate in his eyes. Bobby was tall and thin. His face showed his pain. His eyes smiled, but underneath there was such brokenness. Bobby worked at the Yacht Club at Disney World. Michael Jordan and the Olsen twins were among the hundreds of celebrities he met. Bobby chose not to deal with the abuse we endured, instead he used alcohol and women to cover up his pain. He made everyone feel like they were one of the elite. He didn't care what you had or how you looked. Outer appearances meant nothing to Bobby. As our protector, he wanted us to see that another world existed. After 34 years of covering up his pain, our protector took his life. My heart still feels the sting. He left behind his son who was only a baby at the time. For years, I wondered if Bobby made it to heaven. Then, the Lord showed me something in a dream. There will be more on that later in the book.

The second youngest sibling is Paul. We call him P. J. At 5' 8", he has a thin frame and a worn face, but his eyes are bright. Paul is everybody's friend. He and his wife Wendy have two boys. P.J. always tested the boundaries as a kid. On one occasion He locked me in the basement. I panicked to the point that I broke the basement window. I still have the scar on my right hand to prove it. I could never understand how I got in trouble for breaking the window, yet he didn't for locking his younger sister in the basement. He would say that it was because he was mom's favorite. Mom always smiled and said we were all her favorite. He was the baby for three years before I came along. As older brothers sometimes do, I remember him being physical with me. Bobby would come in and put him in his place. Paul is friends with everyone.

I was born Monday, April 14, 1975. It was a cold wintery day with a high temperature of only 40 degrees in Mishawaka, Indiana. Saint Joseph Hospital was the local community hospital. It was the same hospital where my grandmother had been a nurse. Many years before, she had rushed my grandfather there after she hit him over the head with a frying pan while he was sleeping. Was this where it all started?

I took my first breath and was already in a fight for my life. Poison ran through my veins. I was already appointed once to die.

Hebrews 9:27 (NIV) Just as people are destined to die once, and after to face judgement.

I was in a battle I was ill equipped to win. Straddled between two worlds...the world of flesh where sin and lust run rampant destroying everything within reach and my spirit man. The God breathed life into me. The seeds placed in me by my Creator were already determined to lead me to my destiny.

As a newborn, I was unaware of the heartache or the terror that would soon surround me. I was clueless to the extreme poverty, physical, mental and sexual abuse I would endure. I didn't know that demons of drugs and alcohol lived inside the man that was supposed to protect and love me. The safe environment of the hospital was short lived. For the next 16 years regardless of what my address was, the environment was the same.

I was born to Robert Allen Beck, Sr. At the age of 30, he was diagnosed with bipolar disorder. He lost his mother at a young age and was raised by his father. His mental disease made it difficult to stay employed. He was prone to extreme mood swings that often led to physical and sexual abuse. He would medicate himself with drugs and alcohol which only made everything worse. My mother, Barbara W. Winifred was 27 years old when I was born. She was a waitress at Big Bear Restaurant, a local diner near our house. Her mother was a catholic nurse and her father was an army veteran who was an alcoholic and prone to violence.

I had a house full of family to welcome me to my new home. Four sisters and two brothers were there anxious to take me in their arms and take care of me. Little did they know, they were to be guardians as much as my siblings.

I was brought into a home that smelled like cigarettes. Our refrigerator empty and our clothes were not washed. The nine of us lived in a two-bedroom rental home. Seven kids slept in one room, our parents in another. We were the epitome of poverty, yet our parents always had money for cigarettes and drugs.

Julie was in charge of the daily care of us. At ten years old, she took on the role of my parent and guardian. She rushed to feed me, change me and hold me when I cried. She snapped the others into line if she felt they were putting me in harm's way. Not realizing it, I was being cared for by the guardians that God put in place for me. Throughout my life, they were there ready to protect me from what was to follow.

I have all but forgotten the first years of my life. I can only recall my youngest memories through the eyes of my siblings. The stories of horror and heartbreak. This is where the secrets and lies started. This is where we learned to obey and do what our father wanted or he would beat our mother as punishment. This is where we learned to be polite, to smile and never to talk about what was happening behind closed doors.

Most of the homes we lived in were rentals. The homes that don't require credit checks. The paint was peeling, and the messy yards had old cars out front. During the day, the adults who were out of work would sit around drinking and doing drugs. Teenagers skipping school could hang out, have sex and drink. Our house was one of the houses where kids would go. Parents didn't ask us where we were going to college. No, no one ever asked, "What do you want to be when you grow up?".

Our neighbors varied, and we had many. One rental house was across from a shopping center. My teacher lived nearby at the corner of our street. She was very strict compared to the other teachers. In a dare from my brother, I went up to her door prepared to ring the bell then run. As I approached the door, I saw that only a glass door separated me from the inside of her house. There she stood in front of the door cleaning her window. My eight-year old eyes locked on her. "Tracie, what do you need?" I confessed how I was dared to ring her bell, then run away. Her look said, "go ahead" with a smile. So, I rang the doorbell and ran back to the house as quickly as my legs would carry me. Ding, Dong, Ditch was one of the games we would play outside. The men of the neighborhood would come outside and play kickball with us in the evenings. We had fun summer nights. Because there were seven of us, we always had plenty to play team sports.

In the summer, we went camping. It was not an ordinary camp. This camp was for nudists. The first rule was no bathing suits in the pool. Sixty and seventy year-old men watched us as they sat exposed for all to see. I hated going there. I wanted to run and hide. Writing this now stirs up the emotions of how afraid and uncomfortable I felt. I am forced to confront the fact that this was a place where children were exposed to incest and terror. On the gate outside we were "naturalists" on the inside we helpless to defend ourselves against what was happening.

In the fall, we would go back to school. I always enjoyed the peace that school offered. This is where I would receive the one meal I would eat that day. Some years, I would have that one teacher that would speak life into me. Unlike everyone else, they wouldn't look down on me or on my dirty clothes. They didn't ask about my missing homework assignments. Did they somehow know that when I went home what I would experience was more than enough punishment? Could they tell that something wasn't quite right? Could they hear what the Holy Spirit was telling them?

Hebrews 4:13 (NIV) Nothing in all creation is hidden from God's sight. Everything is uncovered and laid bare before the eyes of Him to Whom we must give account.

A million times I wondered why our mother didn't take us away...why someone didn't help us. Looking back, I remember moments of interventions gone bad. My siblings would reach out and tell other adults what was going on. It never went well. My parents would say they were lying and it would be dismissed. Then we would all be left to face the consequences.

When I was in elementary school, the local church Sunday School bus came through the projects where we were lived. We would all get picked up for Sunday School which we loved. Waiting for us on the bus was a snack, and when we got to the church we learned about God and His Son, Jesus, and that we should pray. That time was enjoyable as we sat in a safe place where we felt a new kind of love that didn't hurt. Great seed was planted into our lives. When the church bus stopped coming, our temporary refuge was over. There were no more weekend snacks. Our parents' break from us was over, and our break from them was over.

There were many moments of hunger growing up. A few stand out more than others do. Being poor and hungry is not uncommon. Sometimes we had money, but we were not fed. Once we all waited upstairs with empty stomachs while our parents ate lobster. One night, dad came and woke us up at 3:00 am. He was furious and screaming because one of us had eaten some Jell-O my mom had made. No one confessed that night, so we all suffered for what equated to a ten-cent treat.

Psalm 107:9 (NLT) For He satisfied the thirsty and fills the hungry with good things.

Even in chaos, we can find moments to remember fondly. If our body cooperates, we can begin to imagine what a perfect childhood would look like. We loved going to my mom's mother's house. Grandma Johnson was a catholic nurse who believed in loving discipline. She knew we were always hungry. There was something about having food and feeling safe that made me drift off as I laid down on the soft comforter atop of her double bed. I knew I was safe at her house. She hated my father and knew the allegations of abuse were true. She saw the pain in all our eyes. I can only imagine how it must have broken her heart to see us and the life we were living. How was my mother able to look into her eyes knowing it was with her permission that the abuse was taking place? How could she play the victim for so long? My mom divorced my dad three times. It was never because of what was happening to us. She would leave when she got tired or mad. She always ended up back with him. It was never about us.

I love my mom very much. I've learned to accept that people do the best they know how to do at the time. The hope is that as they learn better, that they will do better.

James 1:5 (ESV) If any of you lacks wisdom, let him ask God who gives generously to all without reproach, and it will be given him.

In the summer of 1988, Rachel Foster and I were best friends. We went everywhere together. Spending the night at her house meant staying up late, telling stories and talking about cute boys. I never wanted to go home, so I would stay at her house whenever I could. Her parents invited me to come to live with them and I wanted to, but I knew my parents would have never let me.

The Fosters knew there was something wrong at our house. They could never have imagined how bad it was. Rachel's parents took me to church like the old school bus did. Her parents were good country folks. Christian Country music and Acapella Vocal Band (AVB) played on the radio of their van. Once Rachel and I went to an AVB concert and had a blast. The Fosters weren't perfect, but I felt safe with them. I would shower and eat. Before school, I would help Rachel with chores like putting the dishes away, so she wouldn't get in trouble. Mrs. Foster would drive us back and forth to practice at the 4-H fair. I was free to be a kid. Rachel and I were in 4-H, the Drama Club, and we went to Youth Group. We could be and do anything in our small pretend world. Rachel decided she wanted to change her name to Raquel, so she did. For the entire year she referred to herself only as Raquel. We entered a 4-H clown competition at the local county fair and won. We went all the way to State to compete. Hanging out at the fair was fun, and it was there that I met my first real boyfriend. He sold cokes at the fair. We had a fun innocent summer that year.

Rachel was strategically placed into my life by God. I didn't realize it at the time though. She and her family would alter the course of my life. Every year the Foster's church offered a Youth Camp. I would never have been able to go, but the Fosters offered to pay my way, so my parents let me go. By far, that week became one of the best memories of my childhood. It was nothing like the "camp" I went to before. It was great! We played games, swam in the lake and sang by the campfire. It was there that I raised my hand when the time came and accepted Jesus into my heart. It was at the moment a seed was planted that I wouldn't see bloom for years to come.

John 14:6 (NIV) Jesus said to him, I am the way, the truth and the life. No one comes to the father except through me.

How different would my life have been had I not felt the tug of the Holy Spirit that night. I let Him pull me in the direction of my Savior.

By the time I was in high school, I was practicing what I seen my entire life. From the time I was a young girl, I was taught that sex was love...love was sex. My body was to be used to get love. How could someone not realize that one can have sex and it have nothing to do with love? You may read that and think that is so silly. How could someone not realize that you can have sex and it not have anything to do with love? I mean, it's instinctive to know that you wait to get married to have sex right? Walk my journey, and try and see it from my eyes. I was violated way before I ever went to church. I never had a choice with whom I would have my first experience. That choice was stolen from me. That choice was snatched out of my hands from someone who had no authority to take it.

Like a thief sneaking in and taking something that was never meant to be theirs.

Exodus 20:15 (NIV) You shall not steal.

I have great compassion for children who come from abusive backgrounds. I feel the way the world looks at them and judges them. They should have known better than to make the choices they did--wondering why they are kids with kids. But, they are trapped in a cycle. Without a community stepping up, they will stay in that cycle and their children will be destined to follow. Next time you are tempted to judge, remember my story and ask yourself what you can do to plant a seed of life into that child of God.

In my search for love, I had a lot of boyfriends before I was married. At the age of thirteen, I found myself wishing that I could get pregnant so that someone would love me. I would have someone to love. I wanted a baby but not the husband. I never wanted marriage. It did not matter that I couldn't take care of myself much less an infant. It didn't matter that my life would have been a disaster. I wanted to love and to be loved.

I never asked much of the boyfriends I had. I was easy to get along with and didn't ask for much in return. I somehow remained positive and worked hard. My choices were not the best when it came to young men. The hard-working, kind, respectful type of fellows weren't given the time of day. I chose what I knew. The ones that loved me for what I could give them. I was attracted to the guy who would cheat and talk down to me. In the middle of this, how did Jesus find me?

Psalm 139:13-16 (ESV) *For You formed my inward parts; You knitted me together in my mother's womb. I praise You, for I am fearfully and wonderfully made. Wonderful are Your works; my soul knows it very well. My frame was not hidden from you, when I was being made in secret, intricately woven in the depths of the earth. Your eyes saw my unformed substance; in Your book were written, every one of them, the days that were formed for me, when as yet there was none of them.*

Chapter 2 Application: Let God help you grow in the courage to trust people again. Choose to let people plant seeds into your life. Those seeds can produce a harvest decades later. Take a second to remember the people that God has already planted in your life, and thank Him for always remembering you. Remember the good people in this world that were placed by God to help you in your journey. Build up the courage to let them do what they know they were placed in your life to do. Thank God for sending people who took the time to notice you, notice your pain, knowing they watered the seed that God planted in you. You may think that the ground in your life is too hard to see a breakthrough for your harvest, but God has miracle power that picks up in your weakness and does something with your life that you can't explain. God hasn't forgotten you. You may be at the beginning of your healing journey so keep putting one foot in front of the other, Refuse to stop, and you will get there! God is well able to finish what He started in you.

Philippians 1:6 (NIV) Being confident of this, that He who began a good work in you will carry it on to completion until the day of Christ Jesus.

CHAPTER 3

HELLO BIG FELLA

I remember when I was first introduced to Eric. He was twenty years old. Both his eyes and his biceps were big. I was a server at Azar's Restaurant. He was 5' 10" with dark black hair. During the week, he worked out of town doing steel construction which gave him amazing arms. While in town one weekend, he came into Azar's and was seated in my section. I was 120 pounds and stood 5' 7" with my brown hair and hazel eyes. The law of attraction was at work that day. God had a plan and a purpose for these two young kids. Troy, Eric's friend, knew...he knew Eric liked me right away. "Don't I know you from somewhere?", Eric asked with Troy's approval. Sorry, I was not impressed. He was polite but cheesy. I liked his friendliness, but I was there to work, to make money, and I had just broken up with my boyfriend.

At that time, I was living with my parents on Olive Street in South Bend. With no transportation of my own, I took a cab to and from work. I finished my shift and left Eric and Troy to be taken care of by my co-worker. I stepped outside to wait for my cab. As I waited, I lit up a cigarette. Eric later told me that when he saw me light up, he was disappointed. He thought I was a good Christian girl. Unfortunately, I had picked up bad habits early. I started smoking at thirteen and drinking well before then.

I enjoyed waitressing, but what I liked more was making money. I stashed my tip money in a plastic Cheeto can. I wanted my money with me and not in the bank. There was something I wanted. I didn't know what it was. I just knew I needed to have money for when it showed up. I used the skills I was taught my whole life. Smile, flirt and be approachable.

I would come home from work to the smell of marijuana and pornographic movies playing on the television. My father didn't care that everyone in the house could see them. I hated them and everything they represented. I would make a bowl of ice cream or some macaroni and cheese and go to my bedroom and shut the door.

The next weekend, Eric called me at work. "Did you get the flowers I sent you?" Another cheesy pickup line, I thought. "I ordered you roses from Michelangelo's...didn't you get them?" He was still working out of town, so I thought I would never hear from him again, so I politely ended the call. The next day when I came into work, my manager told me that someone had dropped off some flowers for me. I went and looked, and there was a vase of flowers complete with a ribbon. Eric had called his mother and asked her to bring me flowers. She left them with my boss since I was not there. It was a good move on his part. He instantly gained points with my coworkers.

The next time he was in town, I agreed to go out with him on a group date. He was an hour late so my cousin and I were ready to go when he pulled up. I had failed to mention that I lived in South Bend, so he had been driving around Lincoln Way in Mishawaka. When he came to the door, my dad was smoking pot like it was something everyone does. Eric had to be wondering what he had gotten himself into.

Our first stop was the pool hall where we met up with his friends. We had a great time and laughed a lot. Later we grabbed some dinner before Eric drove me back to South Bend. He was a perfect gentleman. He opened my door and didn't try to kiss me or to even hold my hand. We wanted to see each other again the next day, but I already had plans to go to the Mishawaka Memorial Day parade with my extended family. So, I invited him to meet me there. Afterwards, we said goodnight, and I walked into the house. That was Sunday, May 24, 1992.

Looking back, I began to see a glimpse of Eric's character. From the outside, he was broad and strong. He had the look of a protector. But, there was so much more that God had placed in him. Would he be the one that would guide this broken waitress in her God-given destiny.

2 Thessalonians 3:3 (NIV) But the Lord is faithful. He will establish you and guard you against the evil one.

The next day we met at the Memorial Day Parade on Main Street in Mishawaka. My whole family was there. Grandma was in her lawn chair, and the kids sat on a blanket near the curb. As the floats passed, they riders threw candy. Everyone waved flags supporting the veterans as they marched by. After the parade, we had lunch at Pizza Hut before he took me back to South Bend.

We were growing closer and things were getting serious when my old boyfriend began calling. He wanted to get back together. I had dated him for over a year so to me he was everything that was familiar. We had similar upbringings. He was from the same neighborhood, and we had the same friends. Then, there was Eric. He was raised in church his whole life. He was a perfect gentlemen with strong convictions. We had absolutely nothing in common. He had lived in the same home almost his whole life. He and his friends went to church together. I needed insight, and God gave it to me that night. I had never been interested in finding a husband, but I knew in that moment that Eric would make a good husband.

We continued dating and eventually things got really serious. One night at the fair, we were at the top of the double Ferris wheel. We both loved rides. He liked the ones that whirled around and I liked the ones that would go high and fast. While we waited for the passengers below to unload, I rocked our car back and forth as we talked. We talked about having a baby together. We both had already dropped out of high school. I had stopped going on my own, and Eric's dad had given him permission to work full time when he was 16 years old.

Ray Douglas Hunsberger was born on May 18, 1993. Nothing was planned, and I was scared. The labor was hard as Ray was stuck in the birth canal. It took a staff of people to bring him safely into this world. I was18 years old when I delivered him. Six weeks later, Eric did what he knew in his heart was right, and we got married. I was in love with our new baby, but we were immature and had nothing to fall back on...not a diploma, not a career. But, we had made a commitment to each other and to this little life we had created.

Romans 8:28 (NIV) And we know that God causes all things to work together for good to those who love God, and who are called according to His purpose.

I was a mom a month after I turned eighteen and married just six weeks later. I look at my daughters today. At that age, prom and graduation were their priorities. Their biggest concerns were choosing a prom date and wondering what their hair and makeup should look like. I, on the other hand, was waking up to a newborn. I often wondered if his successes or failures would be influenced by the choices I would make. I had come from a life of abuse and addiction. I had never experienced what it meant to be raised properly.

I remember bringing Ray home from the hospital. His little head was tilted sideways in the car seat. We had to wrap a blanket up and tuck it beside his head to keep it straight. No one tells you how emotional motherhood is going to be. And, by emotional I mean exhilarating, exhausting and gut-wrenching. My dream of motherhood was romantic. I envisioned a beautiful nursery and being showered with gifts while playing and laughing with my newborn for hours.

There were moments when I found myself wondering why I was in such a hurry to become a mom in the first place...especially at 3 am. There I was a child myself. I was determined to care for this little person. I had a duty, and feeding him at 3 am was what I was supposed to do. Other times, I found myself mad at the whole situation.

Motherhood was a pretty life-altering experience, and for me it all happened really fast. Just a few weeks before Ray was born, I could sleep in as late as I wanted and go to bed when I was tired. Weeks later, I found myself without time to even get a good shower. I knew nothing about cooking. The first meal I prepared was Hamburger

Helper that even the dog wouldn't eat!

I learned much through this stage. One of the biggest lessons was that it was okay that I didn't enjoy motherhood every second of every day. It was okay that I was tired and didn't know how to cook. I was doing pretty good considering. I believed God would help me along the way, and He did. He taught me what I didn't know and got us all safely to the next level. In fact, He had already planted people in my path to make sure we would get to the next level. All I had to do was listen to His voice.

Psalm 71:17 (NASB) O God, You have taught me from my youth, And I still declare Your wondrous deeds.

In June of 1993, Eric was only twenty years old. He was working construction. Ray woke us every two hours to feed. Eric and I would take turns sleeping on the couch so that one of us would get a good night's sleep. Eric did a great job balancing work and the new baby. Ray and I spent the day together which was quite different from what I was used to. I wasn't used to being alone. If Ray slept too long, I would wipe a damp washcloth across his feet to wake him up. I loved to play with him. He was beautiful with his brown eyes and brown hair. My heart melted. I wanted to be a great mother for him. I wanted him to have a chance.

Eric's parents were a big help. They provided us with a place to rent right across the street from their home. They went to church every week. If we missed a church service, his dad would let us know that he noticed our absence. At the time, it felt controlling. Later, I realized he knew that centering our lives around Christ would make us successful. Eric's mom was an example of a good wife and mother. While a lot of people judged us, his mom never did. She helped us plan our wedding. She handled every detail and even made our wedding cake. I wore a borrowed wedding dress, but the day was perfect to me. She made it that way.

Eric's mom loved her family like I had never seen anyone do before. She always had dinner on the table and would drop everything whenever her family needed her. We knew if we were low on groceries, we were welcomed there for dinner. She was a phenomenal cook and loved to share her creations with us. Ray was the apple of their eyes. I think Ray reminded them of Eric. She was my go-to source, and thankfully she was just across the street. She knew everything about raising children and was eager to share her wisdom.

I was often confused by the love that I saw her give her family. She wasn't always treated in the manner she deserved, but she always walked in grace. My own experience with family made me want to stand up for her when she wouldn't stand up for herself. Even though my mom hadn't lived it, she made sure I knew that I didn't need a man. She wanted me to remember that I should never let a man misuse me or treat me badly.

This family was different. When conflicts arose, no one walked away. No one filed for divorce or ran into another's arms for comfort. They stuck it out even when things went wrong. I saw this as a weakness, a flaw. I wanted Eric's mom to be strong like me. I wanted her to walk away so that no one could mistreat her. All along, God was teaching me about another kind of love. It is the kind of love that showed me Eric's mom was much stronger than I. I was the weak one. She knew her strength came from Christ. She was His.

Luke 6:28 - 36 The Message (MSG) To you who are ready for the truth, I say this: Love your enemies. Let them bring out the best in you, not the worst. When someone gives you a hard time, respond with the energies of prayer for that person....I tell you, love your enemies. Help and give without expecting a return. You'll never - I promise - regret it...Our Father is kind; you be kind.

During the first year of Ray's life, Eric and I argued a lot. He wanted to go play basketball, and I felt alone in bearing the parenting responsibilities. We were two immature kids who were trying to be parents. Most days I felt like a failure. We made it to Ray's first birthday which was a fun family celebration. Both sides were there. He was growing up fast, and we were thankful for family. Eric's sister, Tina had five kids so someone was always there to play with Ray. It was a nice break in our day to spend afternoons with them.

In the fall of 1994, I decided to get my GED. Eric's sister Tina had gotten hers, and I wanted to do the same. After setting my mind to it, I followed her example and took my test on October 20,1994. It was a good achievement and it inspired Eric to do the same. On January 10, 1995, Eric received his GED. It was a small step in the right direction...the first of many.

Proverbs 27:17 (NIV) As iron sharpens iron, and one person sharpens another.

Eric and I were attending church in Elkhart, Indiana when we learned I was pregnant again. It was the church where his parents were members. I felt welcomed there in spite of my insecurities. I never felt like I had on the right outfit, and there was a lot I didn't understand. People prayed with their eyes closed and their hands lifted. When I asked the Pastor why, he explained how it helps them focus on God and to shut out distractions. The Pastor's wife was great to talk to as well. We often worked in the nursery together which gave us time to talk and share. I shared with her my frustration about the way things were going in my life. I couldn't understand why every time I was working hard, it seemed that everything would go wrong. She explained that we have an enemy who doesn't want to see us succeed and that it's not that we are doing something wrong. She went on to say that the attacks can also come because we are doing things right, and the enemy hates that. She was one of many women in the church that I enjoyed getting to know. These women were not what I expected. They were funny and down to earth. At the women's retreat, they told jokes and pranked each other. It reminded me of my sisters, and looking back I know they were planted just for me by God.

On October 19, 1995, I was sitting on the living room floor playing with Ray when my sister Barbie came over. It was her birthday and she was hoping this new baby girl would be born that day. She felt my tummy as she did anytime she was around a pregnant belly. She looked at me and said, "Tracie, you are in labor!" I looked like her like she was crazy. She repeated herself, "Tracie, you need to go to the hospital. You are in labor!" For some reason, Eric and I were not concerned, so we casually got ready and drove to the hospital. I was put on a temporary table as I waited for the room to be readied. The new baby was not aware I was waiting for a room so she entered the world two hours after Barbie stopped by. I am thankful that she came by, or I may have had that baby right in the living room.

I was twenty years old and the proud mom of a two-year-old son and a newborn daughter with brown hair and the biggest blue eyes. We named her Shy Ann Hunsberger. I made sure she was dressed in pink from the day she was born. Barbie was very excited to have a niece to share her birthday. Shy had an independent spirit. As she got older, she would find a toy and play by herself. On her first birthday, we celebrated by having both of our families over. I had ordered a princess cake for my special princess. My mother had picked out a very special Notre Dame cheerleader outfit that fit her just right. The cake was beautiful, and I was excited to share this milestone with everyone. Shy sat in her high chair as I held the cake while we sang Happy Birthday. When I leaned down to let Shy blow out her candle, the cake slid right off the tray and onto the floor. Thankfully, we captured this priceless moment on a home video. You can hear us singing, "Happy Birthday to Shy Ann. Happy Birthday to you OHHHHHH!"

This was a happy time in our lives. I loved to dance with Shy and Ray as we cleaned house on Saturday mornings. Shy was on one hip and Ray on the other. We would spin around and rock back and forth to the music we had playing. They would laugh and smile at each other. Shy would shake her booty as she held her bottle in her teeth. It was these simple things that made us happy. Our life was not perfect, but there were moments of pure joy...moments when we could just dance.

Ecclesiastes 3:1-4 New Living Translation (NLT) A time for Everything . For everything there is a season, a time for every activity under heaven. A time to be born and a time to die. A time to plant and a time to harvest. A time to kill and a time to heal. A time to tear down and a time to build up. A time to cry and a time to laugh. A time to grieve and a time to dance.

Our lives were evening out. We were going to church and growing up. We served in the middle school class at church and volunteered at Vacation Bible School. We enjoyed serving whether it was leading the Hallelujah Party in October or emptying trash cans. I wanted to serve the Lord however I was able.

Winters in Northern Indiana were harsh, but we managed to have fun. We would put Ray and Shy in their snowsuits to play while we shoveled the driveway. Ray would ride his bike, build snowmen and run with our boxer Sammy (who was named after Samson, the strongman in the Bible). We rented our house from Eric's parents. It was an older home situated on a couple of acres. For fun, we would go into the woods on an adventure and pretend we were listening for wild animals. Money was tight, but we always managed to have fun.

Eric usually got home from work around 5:00. We would all be so excited. The kids would run to the door screaming his name with huge smiles on their faces. One Saturday in 1997, Eric walked in and said he wanted to go to Bible College. Our Pastors had gone to college and spoke highly of their experience. It seemed Eric had put some thought into it. He said that if we were going to do it, it was the right time. We had the money and we could move into an apartment in Tulsa.

I, on the other hand, did not share in the excitement. I was pregnant with our third child. The idea of moving twelve hours away did not make sense to me. Eric was being called to ministry. He said if he ever went to Bible College, this school would be the only place he would consider. It started when he was growing up and his dad owned a mechanic garage. Each day at 11:30, they would pull up a couple of milk crates and listen to radio program where the teacher would speak on faith and love. He remembers it well and seeds were planted in Eric that would later produce fruit.

Galatians 6:9 (NIV) Let us not lose heart in doing good, for in due time, we will reap if we do not grow weary.

In a few short months, we were packed and on our way. We found an apartment in Tulsa and Eric took a job working as a manager. Every day we would watch Eric leave for class, come home for lunch, and then be off to work. It was a very lonely time for me.

Our third child, Alyssa was born in October of 1997. Unlike my other two, Alyssa was a fussy baby. She was often inconsolable and cried not matter what I tried to do. I would hold her, sing to her and rock her. Nothing would work. I wondered if she was able to sense how unhappy I was.

A few weeks after Alyssa was born, I had a tubal ligation. We were satisfied with our family. I wasn't sure how I felt about having a surgery to prevent children, but I knew our hands were full. If God wanted me to have another child, this surgery would not stop him. It wasn't long after my surgery that I began telling with Eric that I wanted him to take us back home. Once the decision was made, Eric met with his advisors and explained the situation. They were gracious and let him know that he would be welcomed if he ever decided to come back. So, once again, we packed the moving truck and headed out on a twelve-hour trip. On the drive, I told Eric that I would never move back to Oklahoma. We both felt like failures, as if we failed both God and our families.

Psalm 34:18-19 (NAS) The LORD is near to the brokenhearted, And saves those who are crushed in spirit.

Back into one of Eric's parents' houses we went. Broken and not sure how to move forward, Eric stayed up all night. How could he pick himself up after telling everyone what his plans were only to realize they didn't work out. We were back home with no jobs and no income. We scheduled a meeting with our pastors to discuss what had taken place. Eric explained that he wanted to try to back the next fall, but I was very determined not to ever go back to Tulsa. At our meeting, I let everyone know I would not consider going back to Oklahoma unless we were completely out of debt. At the time, we were $10,000.00 in debt. That could have been a million dollars in my mind. In my eyes, we would never get that paid off, so I was safe from ever having to consider it. They advised us to sit still, stabilize then to follow the peace. While that sounded good to me, Eric was so discouraged. He felt like he would never see the dream that was in his heart.

Thankfully, we both found jobs. I worked at a Christian bookstore doing sales and events. Eric went back to work as a service technician. Between our jobs and raising our three children, we stayed busy. I found my job rewarding. I went to concerts and held training session on the Vacation Bible School curriculum for the local churches. It was a chance for me to meet people. One Pastor I met shared that he had never read the Bible. As our conversation continued, I realized he had not experienced the Word for himself. He was leading a congregation, but had never experienced what it was like to taste the Word. In that moment, my heart grew for those who are trusting their leaders to show them what they don't know.

We were working hard and planting seeds. Things were looking up. We found a great deal on a home and purchased it on a land contract. A year later, we were able to finance it through the bank. Right after that, I was given the opportunity to take a computer and a business class. Eric's mom owned a licensed daycare, so with the kids were in Grandma's capable hands, I jumped on it. It was a good time. We enjoyed working on the house and spending time with the kids. My sister lived close by so, we could visit often. There was so much to do. We rode bikes, visited the park and went on adventures like we did before.

As our family grew, so did our relationship with the Lord. I enjoyed our Sundays at church even though I struggle with letting go and worshipping with all I had. I watched as others raised their hands in praise. I wanted to know why they were doing that. Little by little after getting an explanation from the Pastor, I began to let go. It was a slow process, but as I began to let myself go in worship, I saw the need for God to heal me of my past wounds. The more I opened my hands in worship, the more I wanted to drop the baggage I had been carrying. I went forward at the next altar call, crying and asking Him to heal me...heal me from the abuse that I could not understand.

Philippians 1:6 (NLT) And I am certain that God who began the good work within you, will continue His work until it is finally finished on the day when Christ Jesus returns.

As most mothers do, I was burning the candle at both ends. One day when in class, I began feeling sick. I made an appointment with my doctor to see what was going on. Thinking it could be an ulcer, I blamed it on going to school and raising three kids. I did feel like I was under a lot of pressure. After a short examination, he said, "Maybe you are pregnant." To which, I replied, "I can't be pregnant...I had my tubes tied!"

How could that be. I had put that stage of my life behind me. I was focusing on my health. I was working out two hours a day. I was healthy, strong and happy like never before. I went straight to the convenience store bought a pregnancy test, and saw the double lines that confirmed what the doctor suspected. All I could think to do was to call the doctor back. Jenny, who had known me for years answered. I cried, "Jenny, the test came back positive". I heard her compassion as she replied, "Oh, Tracie, come back in."

The doctor explained that pregnancy after a tubal ligation is not only possible, but could potentially be dangerous. Tubal pregnancies can result. I called Eric crying, and explained the situation. He met me at the hospital for the ultrasound that would let us know if our baby was safe and where it should be.

It wasn't long after the warm jelly was applied, that we heard the heartbeat of our child. The baby was in a safe spot and would arrive in May of 2000.

I was 24 years old and pregnant for the fourth time. When that reality hit, I blamed Eric. I don't know why, but I needed to blame someone for this. He wanted to console me. He reminded me that babies are gifts from God and that he always thought I looked beautiful when I was pregnant. That didn't make me any happier at that moment, although writing it today warms my heart.

We had worked so hard. We had gotten our GED's and I was taking courses at a computer and business school. There was so much I was learning and was grateful for Sonia, my instructor. She took extra time with me so that I could master the interviewing skills we were learning. I learned the importance of making eye contact and how to answer basic interview questions. She would set up mock interviews for us with women who owned businesses. We were graded on how well we did, and I was told that each of the business owners would have hired me. My hard work and heeding the advice I was given got me a job offer from the school I was attending. After graduation, I was offered a job giving the Microsoft Office tests, answering the phones and welcoming new students. The $7.50 an hour wage I got was more than I had ever made. It was all going well until one day.

I had been there for several months when the school decided that it would be good to have cookies for the students. They asked me to make them. Did they not know that I was not a waitress or a Subway employee? Did they not know how hard I had worked? It was not to make cookies. At that moment, I allowed my pride to take over. How could they ask me to go back to a place that I had grown past? I have found that sometimes my head will try to destroy what God is trying to do in my life. In my mind, making cookies would have taken me backwards. Even good common sense would tell you that was improbable, but the thought was so powerful. I reacted and left a job I was so happy with.

Romans 12:2 (KJV) And do not be conformed to this world, but be transformed by the renewing of your mind, so that you may prove what the will of God is that which is good and acceptable and perfect.

During the day, I would watch preachers on television. I read Christian books on healing from abuse. Testimonies of abuse and renewal spoke to me. Healing services confirmed what I always believed. God does amazing things when you let Him work in your life. Because of the disappointment I felt, my heart was more open to what God was trying to do. I listened more closely and prayed with more intensity. Spring had broken, and my pregnancy was going well. I listened to worship music and focused more and more on loving God.

At six, four and two, Ray, Shy and Alyssa were getting bigger. It was a fun time. We grew vegetables in our small backyard garden. There were extra green beans, tomatoes, cucumbers and lettuce for the raccoons and bunnies. I'm not sure if anyone else understood, but we enjoyed watching the bunnies hop through our garden. It was our own nature channel happening in our back yard. The girls would gather the vegetables by holding the hem of their matching dresses while Ray played on the swing set. They loved working in the garden, and I loved putting flowers from the yard into their hair.

In early May of 2000, I was feeling the start of labor pains. After calling the doctor, we headed to the hospital. When I got into the hospital room, I was injected with something for pain. Within seconds, my entire body went numb. Eric saw the fear in my eyes as I told him I could not move my body. At that moment several members of the medical team left the room. I could not feel my legs. I could not feel anything from my feet to the top of my head. Eric prayed over me as they injected me with another drug. Within seconds, the feeling returned. Whatever it was reversed the paralysis, but I was unable to feel my contractions. Eric and the doctor had to tell me when to push. It was then that we welcomed baby Brittney into the world. She was our little miracle baby. We never planned for her, but she was here now and part of our family. Eric and I had four children under the age of seven. We didn't have everything figured out, but we had God. We knew He would help us.

Jeremiah 33:3 New Living Translation(NLT) Ask Me and I will tell you remarkable secrets you do not know about things to come.

Chapter 3 Application: Maybe you are in a time in your life when you realize that you have sabotaged yourself like I did when I refused to make cookies at the computer and business school. Or you have found yourself in a stage that you thought you had moved beyond like when I found myself pregnant with our fourth child after having my tubes tied. In that moment, I was in tears wondering why this was happening. God has a plan for your life, and He will see it come to pass if you keep moving forward and allow him to shape you into what He created you to become.

If you are feeling overwhelmed today, feeling like you have made a mistake and that your future is hopeless, God says NO, don't give up now. He has a plan, hold on and buckle down. A breakthrough is coming! Keep getting up, keep putting one foot in front of the other and don't focus on what is behind you. Put your eyes on the Lord when you feel overwhelmed. Look for opportunities to enjoy where you are today. God will show you secrets about things that are to come. He will guide you on the path that He has for you. Don't get stuck at this stage. Greater things are coming!

CHAPTER 4

IT'S NEVER TO LATE TO START AGAIN

Isaiah 48:17 (ESV) Thus says the LORD, your Redeemer, the Holy One of Israel, "I am the LORD your God, who teaches you to profit, Who leads you in the way you should go."

It was much like any other day. The kids and I were keeping ourselves busy playing, reading and going on adventures. While the kids were napping, I watched evangelistic television. As I did, God showed me that we should return to Bible school in Tulsa. It made no sense. We were settled in our home. We had done some remodeling and things were going well. But, there was a tug, a strong tug, telling me we should go back to school and attend classes together. Imagine Eric's surprise when I announced that I wanted to go back to Bible school especially after how convinced I was that I would never return to Tulsa. We were finally on the same page!

We began preparing our home to sell as we looked for an apartment in Tulsa. We did not have jobs there, but new something would come up once we arrived. We loaded up the moving truck once again. It was the next step in our journey. We were a bit older and thankfully, out of debt. God honored the desire of our hearts to be out of debt. He had been working behind the scenes all along, and we were now where He had planned for us to be.

Romans 8:28 (NIV) And we know that in all things, God works for the good of those who love Him, who have been called according to His purpose.

This time there was an excitement in the air when we arrived. After checking into the hotel, we drove by the apartment to get a first look. Since we had booked the rental online, we were seeing it for the first time. Sheets, not curtains, covered the windows that were not boarded up. The neighborhood looked much like the apartments I lived in as a child. I wanted to be as optimistic as I could, so I told Eric it would better in the morning. As we drove away, a Broken Arrow police officer drove past us. Realizing he was not buckled, Eric reached over to secure his seat belt. With his lights on, the officer pulled up behind us. With flashlight in hand, he asked, "When did you put your seatbelt on?" Eric replied, "I put it on when I got in the car". The officer looked at Eric again and asked, "Are you sure you want to stick with that story?" "No, I don't", he replied. Eric explained that we were new to the area and had stopped by to see the apartment we had booked online. Without hesitating, the officer let us know that he would not move his family into those apartments. They were too dangerous with drug and criminal activity. He kindly referred us to someone he knew who managed apartments in the area. He sent us on our way after giving Eric a verbal warning about the seat belt.

The next morning, we talked to the manager of the rundown apartment complex. We asked for our deposit then called the number the officer had given. We needed a three bedroom apartment, so as we waited to see what was available, we walked through one of the apartments. They were nice and had a workout room and a pool. With daycare and school payments, we could use some freebies. We were told an apartment with three bedrooms would be coming up for lease, but it would take two to three weeks. We unloaded our moving truck into a storage room the next day and called our good friends, Troy and Taffi. They were pastors who lived an hour away in Sallisaw, Oklahoma. They offered their home to us until our apartment was ready. All we had to do was figure out how to come up with the extra money for the new apartment. Eric knew the answer. He, his dad and his uncle Stephen all had the same model 1986 Kawasaki Eliminator. It was a rare model as it was only in production for two years. He loved that motorcycle, but he knew He wanted to follow God more. Eric had a second chance to follow his dream of going to Bible College. Eric had a choice to make, would he totally sell out for God?

Luke 18:22 (NIV) When Jesus heard this, he said to him, "You still lack one thing. Sell everything you have and give to the poor, and you will have treasure in heaven. Then come, follow me."

Eric eagerly sold his bike to his brother Kevin. It took Kevin and his daughter Deanne twelve hours to drive from northern Indiana to Tulsa to pick up the bike, and I suspect, to help out his little brother.

We settled in to our new apartment and began looking for work. We agreed that whoever was offered the best opportunity would work and the other would stay home. There was a job board in the schools administrative building. I applied with one of the companies and got an interview. Eric was also interviewing with several companies. We both were offered jobs, but we knew only one of us could work. Years before, we heard a speaker at our home church in Elkhart, Indiana speak on faith, money and God's financial system. He spoke on the importance of setting yourself up in a position to be blessed.

Eric had been offered a job with a base pay, and I had been offered a job making a base pay plus commission. We have been taught to look for opportunities to make tips, bonuses, commissions and investments. I never forgot that advice. So when the time came for us to choose, we felt that God could do more with the opportunity I had been given. We would both take on new roles. Eric became a student and stay-home dad, and I became a student and provider for the family.

The day school started, we knew we were sold out to God's plan. We were filled with excitement and determined to find His perfect will for our lives. We knew that He would take us to places we never could have dreamed to go.

Matthew 6: 33 (NIV) But seek first His kingdom and His righteousness, and all these things will be given to you as well.

Being sold out did not mean it was going to be easy. We had four kids between the ages of eight and two. A typical day involved getting them and ourselves ready, dropping Brittney and Alyssa off, then getting Ray and Shy to school. After that, Eric and I attended our morning classes. On the way home for lunch, we would pick up Brittney at the babysitter's and Alyssa at preschool. After a quick lunch, I would head to work. At around 11:30 pm, I would get home from work then get in some study time before bed.

As long as my days were, Eric was working as hard if not harder. I had always been the primary caregiver. Now he was the one changing diapers, giving baths, cooking, cleaning and doing the laundry. I called him my first night at work to check in. He told me he had yet to make it out of the kitchen! I knew exactly how he was feeling in that moment. Eric did a great job caring for the kids even if the kids didn't always appreciate his strict parenting style. I knew they were safe and well protected while I could not be with them.

The classes we attended together were amazing. We were being taught by some of the best Bible teachers in the world. Eric and I were on the same spiritual page. I received so much revelation during my time in Bible College. One class in particular that I remember was a class on Pneumatology. The instructor broke down the complex issue of faith so that even I understood it. His words were, "When I don't know if I have enough faith for something, I have faith that God loves me enough to take care of the things that concern me." It was that simple yet profound message that I would cling to during some of the hardest times I would later face.

We loved meeting people from all over the world. Raji and Raza were our neighbors from India. We would see them walking the neighborhood or enjoying their yard. Each time, we would wave hello. One day they waved us over so we stopped for a visit. When we got out of our minivan to greet our neighbors, Eric was greeted with a kiss right on the mouth by Raji. Eric's look was priceless. How I wish I had a video recording of the whole thing. Although he was shocked, Eric remained respectful and friendly. They invited us in to drink chai tea. We talked about raising kids and going to Bible School. We invited them to church, and Raza's response was priceless. In his Indian accent, he said, "I do not understand this church. They sit down. They stand up...what is this all about?" I loved his innocent and honest perspective.

At Bible College, everyone takes the same classes the first year. During the second year you chose the specialty classes you would like to take. Eric chose Pastoral Ministry, and I chose Youth Ministry. We broke down into smaller groups to go through our specific areas of study. There was so much I wanted to teach the youth. It was a chance for me to protect them from the mistakes I had made. I had not received the instruction I so wanted to give to them. It was my passion to teach them everything I wish I had learned.

Corinthians 10:13 (NIV) No temptation has seized you except what is common to man. And God is faithful; He will not let you be tempted beyond what you can bear. But when you are tempted, he will also provide a way out so that you can stand up under it

We finally made it to graduation and were so excited to walk down the aisle to get our diplomas. For each of us, it would be our first time walking down the aisle to grab ahold of our diplomas! The week before graduation our families started arriving. Eric's parents and his siblings Matthew and Rebecca came in as well as my mom and sisters, Julie, Barbie, Patty and Kim. Because we had a few days before graduation to spend together, we decided to go to the museum. Alyssa was a little under the weather, but I thought it was from all the excitement of having family in. I pushed her in the stroller even though she was old enough to walk. Later that evening, Alyssa started spiking a fever and within hours was unable to get up on her own. We took her to the emergency room in Broken Arrow. After examining her, it was decided that she needed to be transferred to the hospital in Tulsa.

After a few hours, she was admitted. We knew at that point, we would spend graduation looking after our little girl.

It took three days of running tests to determine what was wrong with Alyssa. As we waited, we didn't expect to have visitors from school. After all, it was right before graduation. To our surprise, the dean and his wife came to visit Alyssa twice. We also were visited by the church hospital team. They brought Alyssa a "Faith Friend". It was a small kitty beanie that had a faith shield across its shirt. We put it on her IV as a reminder of God's healing power. The tests results finally came in and showed that Alyssa had an extra tube on each of her kidneys. Her condition would require surgery and then medication for the rest of her life.

Our plan was to move back to Indiana after graduation . We had packed up our apartment and loaded the moving truck expecting to leave right after graduation. Eric's parents offered to take Ray, Shy and Brittney back to Indiana so we could be at the hospital with Alyssa. My family stayed behind for a couple of days to give us the family support we so needed. We prayed, the church prayed, and Alyssa used that kitten as a reminder that God had already healed her. Eric asked the doctors if Alyssa could make the drive back to Indiana so that she could have the surgery there. It would make her recovery easier, and we could be back together as a family. The doctors agreed that she could make the trip provided we got her to the doctor immediately after arriving.

Alyssa was still extremely sick during the drive home. We would pull over while she was getting sick. I held her and Eric prayed. We made it home and got Alyssa in to see our family doctor. He reviewed the tests from the hospital in Tulsa and agreed that Alyssa did have an extra tube on each of her kidneys. He decided he would like to run the tests again to get a better view of her situation. We scheduled the tests then went back to meet with the doctor. What came next was nothing short of a miracle. On the first set of tests you could clearly see the tubes. On the second set of tests, they were completely GONE! Alyssa would not need surgery or medication. It was a miracle that we could only attribute to God answering our prayers. Over the next ten years Alyssa would have episodes when she would start to get sick. Whenever that would happen, she would grab her kitty and remember that God is her Healer. That was in May of 2003. We missed another graduation, but God showed us that He is our faithful Healer. What doctors couldn't do, He was faithful to do. All we had to do was put our trust in Him.

Acts 19:11-12 (NLT) God gave Paul the power to perform unusual miracles. When handkerchiefs or aprons that had merely touched his skin were placed on sick people, they were healed of their diseases, and evil spirits were expelled.

Chapter 4 Application: There are times in our lives when God points us in a new direction . Along that path we are given a choice. We can give up, turn back and quit when challenges come our way. Or, we can sell out to God's plan and see where the journey leads. It is worth it to keep moving forward in spite of obstacles that WILL come. Trusting God with childlike faith got us through Bible school . I can look back and see the seeds of faith that were planted in us along the way. Those seeds allowed us to receive both the mental and physical healing we needed. As a result, we were able to plant the same seeds in our children. God always returns our sacrifices with something better. He is a Good Father, and will take care of His children. All we have to do is take a small step forward.

Mark 10:28-31 (NIV) Then Peter began to say to Him, "See, we have left all and followed you." So Jesus answered and said, "Assuredly, I say to you there is no one who has left house or brothers or sisters or father or mother or wife or children or lands for My sake and the gospel's who shall not receive a hundredfold now in this time--houses and brothers and sisters and mothers and children and lands, with persecutions--and in the age to come, eternal life. But many who are the first will be last and the last first.

Deuteronomy 30:19 (NIV) I have set before you life and death, blessings and cursings; therefore, choose life, that both you and your descendants may live.

God has already told us the path we should take, and it is the path of life. We have to pick up our courage one more time and trust him knowing He will never leave us along our journey. He is always there walking hand in hand with us .

Chapter 5

MARRIAGE: IT'S NOT ALL CHOCOLATE AND ROSES

The Bible has a lot to say about marriages and how it should be. But, what do you do when it is going all wrong? What happens when you have a dream together and then one day it feels like that dream has died? When work gets in the way of your relationship. What do you do when you cannot agree on how to discipline and raise children? What do you do when you find yourself not wanting to come home after work? What do you do when the grass begins to look greener on the other side?

Genesis 2:18, 21-24 (NIV) The Lord God said, "It is not good for the man to be alone. I will make a helper suitable for him"...and while he was sleeping, He took one of the man's ribs and closed up the place with flesh. Then the Lord God made a woman from the rib He had taken out of the man, and He brought her to the man. The man said, "This is now bone of my bones and flesh of my flesh; she shall be called "woman", for she was taken out of the man."

For this reason, a man will leave his father and mother and be united to his wife, and they will become one flesh.

The goal is for a man and a woman to be in unity and operating as one. I never understood how this can happen. Two individuals with different backgrounds and different perspectives and are expected to magically become one. Where do they get the power to do this? Sure, they fell in love, but all they did was go through a ceremony. It seemed impossible to me that two people could operate as one unit. That was the case with Eric and me. We came together with my brokenness, scars and distorted views.

In marriages, one or both may be damaged coming in. One may have been abused or abandoned by their parents. They may have seen things that the other did not. Was one of their parents involved in an extra-marital affair? Did one or both experience their parents verbal abuse? Did they see a parent manipulate money? Did they have a depressed parent? Whatever they experienced will likely become their first response to difficulties. I had to overcome those instincts. I had to find a healthy behavior model. This involved retraining myself. I had to search out a mentor to help me grow. I listened to DVD's, read books and weighed all that information against what the Word of God said. I would read scriptures that seemed old fashioned and against what I believed about women.

Ephesians 5:23 -32, NLT: For a husband is the head of his wife as Christ is the head of his body, the church; He gave his life to her Savior. As the church submits to Christ, so you wives must submit to your husbands in everything. And you husbands must love your wives with the same love Christ showed the church. He gave up His life for her to make her holy and clean, washed by baptism and God's word. He did this to present her to Himself as a glorious church without spot or wrinkle or any other blemish. Instead, she will be holy and without fault. In the same way, husbands ought to love their wives as they love their own bodies. For a man is actually loving himself when he loves his wife. No one hates his own body but lovingly cares for it, just as Christ cares for his body, which is the church. And we are his body. As the Scriptures say, "A man leaves his father and mother and is joined to his wife, and the two are united into one." This is a great mystery, but it is an illustration of the way Christ and the church are one.

1 Peter 3:1 - 5 , 7, NLT: In the same way, you wives must accept the authority of your husbands, even those who refuse to accept the Good News. Your godly lives will speak to them better than any words. They will be won over by watching your pure, godly behavior. Don't be concerned about the outward beauty... You should be known for the beauty that comes from within, and the unfading beauty of a gentle and quiet spirit, which is so precious to God ... In the same way, you husbands must give honor to your wives. Treat her with understanding as you live together. She may be weaker than you are, but she is your equal partner in God's gift of new life. If you don't treat her as you should, your prayers will not be heard.

Okay...is anyone else's skin (aka flesh) crawling like mine did?

Doesn't God realize that women are equals, and we can do anything a man can do? Obviously God did not realize who He created us to be. Why would God give this commandment for us to submit to our husbands? Did He really want us to accept our husbands as our authority? HELLO! I married an imperfect man that gets upset and who sometimes doesn't even try very hard.

But wait! Could there be a loophole? Can I get out of submitting to my husband if my husband isn't perfect? What if my husband is not a Christian or he doesn't love me like Christ loved the church? After all, the way that Christ loved the church was perfect. That would be easy...to love someone who was perfect.

As I read more on the subject I learned I am to submit even if he is not a Christian. Are you kidding me??? Why would God say that I can have it all together, but I am still supposed to submit to a man who isn't even a Christian? Did God take a day off when this was written. Perhaps He was multi-tasking and got the topic wrong. Seriously? I have to live with a man every day who is sometimes rude. He forgets to pray for me. Surely, that gets me off the hook! I have to tell him how to fix everything that is wrong in his life. I have to show him what he is doing wrong, so he can fix it so we can move on. What woman wouldn't agree with me on this one.

Yet, as I go on I see that the Word says that by my godly living, he will be won. Regardless of how much I move my mouth and nag him, it will not be the thing that allows God to work on him. He is won to the Lord by my godly living. When I weigh my perception against the truth, I see my words can actually hinder my husband from finding God. That is not a fun pill to swallow. So why would the Lord set it up like this? You would think that we are all set up for failure. After all, does he really need to love me as Christ loves the church...is that even possible for him to do? If I don't submit to him, does that let him off the hook?

Matthew 7:11 - 13 (NIV) So, if you who are evil know how to give good gifts to your children, how much more will your Father in heaven give good things to those who ask Him! In everything, then, do to others as you would have them do to you. For this is the essence of the Law and the prophets. Enter through the narrow gate,. For wide is the gate and broad is the way that leads to destruction and many enter through it.

So wait, I am supposed to treat people as I want them to treat me regardless of how they treat me?

Is anyone else confused?

Even if I had been raised differently, I think I would still have a problem getting my brain around this. Some of the most successful business leaders I have been around would tell you to watch your back, get ahead and protect your future. My upbringing reinforced that thinking. My mother trained me on submission to men and on trusting others. The only person I can count on is myself. I should never put my future in the hands of someone else. I went through a one-hour ceremony. Now, I have to lay down everything I had planned and trust this man to run my life?

Why can't we make a deal with God? We can trust our husbands in certain areas, but in others, not so much. We can take care of everything. This way we can win as a family. Our success is the most important thing after all. No one wants their family living on the streets, right?

We are modern day women. We celebrate that we can do anything. Our opinions are supposed to count and our voices need to be heard. If he speaks, we speak louder. If he messes up, we fix it. We are strong and independent. We are women who can do it all. We can handle any challenge set before us. The sad fact is I thought all of that. I believed I could fix my husband, and that I was the only one who knew the right way of doing things. That's pride at its best!

When we first got married, it was hard for me to reconcile what I had been taught my entire life with what I was learning in church and from my Bible. I can't describe how hard it was to trust my husband to take care of me and to lead us into our future. My reality was that men will let you down and that people in authority will take advantage. Marriage hurts. Those beliefs led me to withhold pieces of myself and build a wall.

I was expected to submit, honor and love. It was at our wedding ceremony that I actually heard those words for the first time. Submit? How about we agree? Honor? Can someone describe that to me because I have never actually seen that. Love? Oh, you mean SEX because that is how I was shown you prove love. Why couldn't we make an agreement to take care of our own stuff? I was in a vulnerable position and could only deal with it by being defensive.

Our first years together were torture for us. We were broke, immature and selfish. Sex made me cry every time we were together. I was damaged on a deep level. I didn't understand the depth of my brokenness, so I pushed on and pretended like I was on top of the world. I put on a strong face and hid behind my smile. I pushed forward, but the pain was unbearable. I wanted to leave every time we had a fight. It was at those times, that I felt worthless and alone. I had put a small band aid on a huge gash. Every time something went wrong, the pain of the past came flooding in. Eric had no clue that he wasn't arguing with an adult. He was arguing with that scared little girl who had been hurt by the world.

If Eric didn't like what I prepared for dinner, I believed I couldn't do anything right. If Eric wanted to spend time with his friends, I believed that something was wrong with me. If Eric told me that I should work on an area of my life, I would hear that I was broken. Because I wasn't raised in church, I was never going to be who he wanted me to be. He would be better off with someone who was like him.

It was hard not to let that hurt show so I made sure I didn't by always pushing myself. The more my world was falling apart, the more successful I became. Eric stood by me through it all, and gave me the room to heal. He was not perfect, but he was faithful and that was enough. He loved me when I was unlovable. He saw me at my worst and yet saw my beauty. He took the punishment for everyone who had hurt me. He watched me heal, and encouraged me along the way. He saw the potential inside of me and showed me that God had big plans for me.

Eric would go on to see me though some of life's toughest challenges. When each one hit, I would push through never allowing myself to heal. I kept smiling and putting band aids on one right over the other. My heart was shattered on the inside. Eric would try to fix whatever was wrong, but I pushed him away. I didn't need or want a love that left me vulnerable. I didn't want anyone to look behind the curtain and see my ugly scars. I could use words better than most. I could build you up or destroy you with my words. If I felt endangered, I would make sure I was protected. I pushed everyone away in the name of self-protection. But, it was not healthy. I can tell you, it will cost you everything. Holding onto one thing may cost you ten. You may find that the person who loves you the most loses a piece of himself trying to protect you.

I had to allow myself to be broken in order to be healed. I had to acknowledge the wounds and work through the process of allowing them to heal. I had to commit to establishing new ways to deal with life and its challenges. God will do a mighty work if you let Him. When it happens, you will find yourself looking back and barely remembering that shadow that used to be you. You will see true strength. The strength that comes from being honest with yourself and with the Lord. You see, we don't know everything, but we serve a God who does. He will bring us safely to the other side of whatever we are going through.

I am going to challenge you to reflect on your past. Look back and reflect on the times when you spirit was crushed or your trust was violated. Go deep into the places that you don't allow anyone else to go. Go to the places that hide behind the walls of safety that you have built. How does it feel when you reflect on those times in your life? How does your heart feel? Do you cry? Do you feel rage? Do you feel lonely? Isolated? Worthless? Write it down and ponder what is causing you to feel that way.

There were times in my life when I was convinced that Eric would let me down. The first time he did disappoint me, I knew it was okay not to ever trust him completely. I was holding him up to an impossible standard. I have let him down hundreds of times in our marriage. Why was I holding him up to such a high standard? By looking back, I recognized that the fear I was feeling was unsubstantiated. The next time I was faced with an issue of trust, I had to make a choice to trust Eric even though it did not come naturally.

In order to be healed, you have to expose your weaknesses. Once you do, ask God to help and guide you. You can seek outside help if you need to talk it through. Then search the Scriptures about how to deal with your issues.

Take unforgiveness: If someone did something to hurt me, I might feel like I have a right to hold a grudge and withhold a part of myself from them. After all, they did something wrong. I have the right to protect myself from any future hurt they may give. I have a right to build a wall. I have an obligation to protect myself. When I go to the Word, I see the roadmap that God gave me for dealing with unforgiveness.

Matthew 6:14-15 (NIV)   For if you forgive others for their transgressions, your heavenly Father will also forgive you. But if you do not forgive others, then your Father will not forgive your transgressions.

Matthew 18:32 -35(NASB) Then summoning him, his lord said to him, "you wicked slave, I forgave you all that debt because you pleaded with me. Should you not also have had mercy on your fellow slave, in the same way, that I had mercy on you?" And his lord moved with anger, handed him over to the torturers until he should repay all that was owed him.

Mar 11:25-26 (NASB) Whenever you stand praying, forgive if you have anything against anyone so that your Father who is in heaven will also forgive you your transgressions. But if you do not forgive, neither will your Father who is in heaven forgive your transgressions.

Luke 6:28-30 (NASB) Bless those who curse you. Pray for those who hurt you. If someone slaps you on one cheek, offer the other cheek also, If someone demands your coat, offer your shirt also. Give to anyone who asks; and when things are taken away from you, don't try to get them back.

I am supposed to forgive people the way that Christ forgave me? How? My heart is broken from the pain they caused, what do I do? Doesn't the Lord know that my heart hurts? How do I let them know that they did something wrong and that I am owed an apology at the very least.

Romans 12:17 -19 (NIRV) Don't pay back evil with evil. Be careful to do what everyone thinks is right. If possible, live in peace with everyone. Do that as much as you can. My friends, do not try to get even. Leave room for God to show his anger. It is written, "I am the One who judges people. I will pay them back."(Deuteronomy 32:35 NIRV) says the Lord.

Luke 23:34 (NIV) Then said Jesus, "Father, forgive them; for they know not what they do." And they parted his raiment and cast lots.

It's never easy on the flesh to choose life. To choose to do what the Word of God says when everything in the flesh wants revenge and wants the person who hurt you to feel as bad as you do. Love chooses life every time. Love seeks someone else's good over your own pain. Jesus was the example of this. He was beaten, spat upon and called a fraud. Yet, he forgave. He did so because he wanted to bring restoration between us and our Heavenly Father. His choice allowed God to work and reveal Himself in a way that we can respond to. Love allows people to hear the Lord speak in their own language. The language of the heart. It is a place where spirits can hear and healing can take place. Let that kind of love be your goal. Choose life for yourself, but also for your enemies. Let your life be the example so they can see God in a new way. We can be like God when we choose to love someone who deserves the harshest sentence. We can give love when it deserves to be withheld. It's never easy, but when you choose forgiveness, you choose life. You set yourself free when you set your enemy free.

All marriages will experience ups and downs. Everyone thinks differently from one another. We express our thoughts and emotions in different ways. Our belief and value systems will likely be different because of how we were raised. Understanding that you will think, act, feel and understand things differently is the first step.

In a Christian marriage, both the man and the woman seek to follow God's plan for their lives and for their marriage. Marriage, when viewed as a covenant before God and man, can create a bond of unity that cannot be separated. That is what that one-hour ceremony was all about.

Mark 10:9 (NIV) Therefore, what God has joined together, let no one separate.

It is a strong bond, a bond of love. When both people are joined together and with God, the bond is powerful and fulfilling. This love comes from God and it allows you to love someone when they are wounded, when they fail and when they hurt you. That one-hour ceremony that seemed insignificant told God that these two will now operate as one with one agenda and one purpose.

Ecclesiastes 4:9 -12(KJV) For if they fall, the one will lift up his fellow: but woe to him that is alone when he falleth; for he hath not another to help him up. Again, if two lie together, then they have heat: but how can one be warm alone? And if one prevail against him, two shall withstand him; and a threefold cord is not quickly broken.

Covenants are throughout the Bible. They are promises and agreements designed to be permanent. Covenants are permanent unions between God and His people. Likewise, a covenant between a man and a woman is considered permanent before God. It is to be sacred and lasting. When our marriage is going through a hard time, we sometimes think about throwing in the towel and leaving. You may say, "If only he or she would shape up and start doing this, this and this. Then, our marriage would be better." Then when nothing changes, you feel like giving up. Sound familiar? If it does, know that you are not alone.

God established a way to have a rewarding and close marriage with your spouse. How? First, you need to draw near to Him and desire to know Him more. Secondly, you have to stop looking to the world for advice on how to have a good marriage and start looking at what the Word of God says. The Bible provides a roadmap for us to have a successful relationship with our spouse. Marriage was God's idea after all. He designed it. He knows exactly what our marriages need in order for them to thrive. His ultimate goal for marriage is for husbands and wives to have oneness that is bound by a holy covenant. It all starts with that one-hour ceremony that I spoke of before.

It is important to remember that our marriages are more than a contract. Contracts can be broken. Unlike a lease on an apartment, our vows are "until death do us part". What that means is it is a holy vow we make before God. The consequences of breaking a covenant before God are very serious. When we see this, we realize that leaving the marriage shouldn't be an easy option.

Ecclesiastes 5:4-5 (GWT) When you make a vow to God do not delay in fulfilling it. He has no pleasure in fools; fulfill your vow. It is better not to make a vow than to make one and not fulfill it.

The reason that Eric and I remain married today is because we made a covenant. It was more than a family tradition or ritual. It's NOT because we felt like staying in it every minute of every day. Many times we could have chosen to walk away and our friends would have agreed that it would have been justified. But, when you are in a covenant, the only solution is to start asking, "What can we do to fix this? What kind of help do we need?". We made our marriage a priority, and we continued to work on it. You never reach a point in a marriage where you can start coasting. You have to always grow and stretch together.

Chapter 5 Application: It can be a challenge to see all the areas that you need to grow as one and as a married couple. God is well able to help you get to the next level in your marriage. Allow yourself to heal from the past and acknowledge the walls you have built. Ask God to help you knock them down one by one. See your spouse as Christ sees him or her. Pray for their weaknesses and submit to your spouse as unto the Lord. As you submit, your spouse will sense that you have lowered your defenses. He will begin to rise to new levels with the Lord's help. God is well able to finish what he has started in your marriage. He will not leave you without help, and He will deliver you into your promised land. At times it can feel overwhelming. You may need to lock yourself in your prayer closet, and cry out to God. That is okay. God loved you before you were created. He knew you, and He set you apart.

Jeremiah 1:5 (NIV) Before I formed you in the womb, I knew you. Before you were born, I set you apart. I appointed you as a prophet to the nations.

Micah 7:7 (NIV) But as for me, I will look to the LORD; I will wait for the God of my salvation; my God will hear me.

God has called you to do great things. First, you have to get into unity with your spouse. You cannot move to the next level until you and your spouse are operating as one. Focus on this area remembering that you made a covenant with each other. It wasn't just a ceremony. It was a pledge that this is the partner you have chosen to help each until death. Quitting is not an option. The only choice you make is to choose life. Together you will empower each other to find and fulfill your divine destinies with the Lord as your guide.

Prayer: Heavenly Father, I lift up those who are calling out to You asking You to heal their hearts and restore their marriages. I thank You that you are hearing their prayers. I thank You that You honor the requests that are in line with the covenants that they made before You when they became united in marriage. I thank You that these couples walk in Your will together. In Jesus Name, I pray. Amen.

CHAPTER 6

SUICIDE DAMAGE CONTROL

It was a busy but fulfilling time in my life. It was 2004, and I was working in the sales department for a publishing company. I was also volunteering with a program with inner city teenage girls and with the children's department at our church in Broken Arrow. The kids were thriving, enjoying their friends and they loved the program at church. On days when I would have liked to skip a Sunday night service, the kids were the ones dragging me to church. I was on the move. I was fulfilled and enjoying my life.

As I headed out the door one morning I grabbed my phone and started walking to the car. It was early November in Tulsa. As I walked down the sidewalk, I turned my cell phone on and was shocked to see hundreds of missed calls from my family in Indiana. I listened to the voicemail and felt my world fall apart. I stood there unable to breathe. I ran back into the house and looked into my husband's eyes. I hung up the phone and fell to the ground. "What happened?", Eric asked. I could barely speak through the tears, "Bobby died last night", I replied with tears running down my face. "How?" Eric asked. "He killed himself." I fell to the floor and started bawling.

I knew that I had to get home to be with my family, so I flew home and Eric drove up with the kids. When I arrived at the South Bend Airport, I saw my dad waiting there to pick me up. We were all in shock. How could this have happened? Bobby was always fun to be around. His smile and energy lit up a room. When Bobby's marriage didn't work out, Eric and I helped Bobby find a place to live. I went over to clean and scrub his new home so he would feel comfortable. He spent a lot of time at our house. Our kids loved it when Uncle Bobby came over. Bobby drank and smoked a lot, but he was always respectful so he left it outside. That was his heart. He cared about his family and was always considerate.

When I was seventeen and pregnant, I didn't know how to deal with all the choices that were staring me in the face. I was unmarried and had just dropped out of high school. I was scared and confused. I took a bus from South Bend to Orlando where Bobby and his wife Crystal welcomed me with open arms. They promised to put me through college and help me in any way they could. He was another guardian in my life. He was not perfect. He knew the mistakes he had made in the past and regretted them. He was my big brother, and I was his little sister. He was loyal to me and committed to helping me clean up any messes that I got myself into. Bobby never made me feel judged. He let me know that I had great potential, and he would help me get there...even if I had made a huge mistake. I stayed with Bobby for four months before deciding it was time to go back to Indiana. He made sure I was safely delivered there too.

When Eric and I were starting out, money was tight. Every year we would take a vacation to see Bobby in Orlando. We would stay with him, and he would give us his employee tickets to Disney World. He would treat us to the Yacht Club Steak House for a fabulous dinner. When I got up at the restaurant, they would brush off my spot and reshape my napkin back into the shape of a swan. For Bobby, it was always about giving people an amazing experience. He believed life should have adventure and great experiences.

For some people, it is easy to pass judgement. Especially when they see that someone is making bad choices. I have lived on the other side of that judgement. I try to give grace and understanding at all costs. I know the side of the story where Bobby tried to reach out to the church. Bobby gave his heart to the Lord at a young age, but made choices that he felt separated him from God. Bobby was broken. He had done things that were wrong, but he reached out and took that first step. It was a step into an unfamiliar place. He was looking for something not even sure what it was. He was an alcoholic, and he came from a background of abuse. The Holy Spirit had beckoned him through the doors. The type of church or the name doesn't matter. I have seen this behavior in many denominations. He walked in, was judged, and turned away by the people inside.

Bobby had a simple heart. He did not get angry at the church who pushed him away. Rejection was what he knew all too well. Sadly, the church gave him exactly what he had always experienced. In that moment, the church was not a refuge or a fortress. It was something that he would move away from. Bobby continued to walk in another direction. He returned to what helped calm the pain inside of him even if it was for a moment. He continued to push the pain down with alcohol. He was numbing the broken pieces deep inside of him. How does anyone deal with trials and suffering without the Lord as his helper? Bobby turned to what he knew he could control. And for him, that was drinking. When Bobby went to a bar, no one pushed him away. His friends were always welcoming with a dance and a smile.

Bobby did not just want to take a drink. His desire for a drink was as strong as his need for food and water. He needed help. He needed a solid support group that included counseling. He needed to talk through the emotions and the pain behind them. He needed a friend, a family and a church to guide him in his relationship with the Lord. He needed a group of people who saw his potential and were willing to put down their agendas long enough to help.

Luke 15:1-7 (NIV) Now the tax collectors and sinners were all gathering around to hear Jesus. But the Pharisees and the teachers of the law muttered, "This man welcomes sinners and eats with them." Then Jesus told them this parable: "Suppose one of you has a hundred sheep and loses one of them. Doesn't he leave the ninety-nine in the open country and go after the lost sheep until he finds it? And when he finds it, he joyfully puts it on his shoulders and goes home. Then he calls his friends and neighbors together and says, "Rejoice with me; I have found my lost sheep." I tell you that in the same way there will be more rejoicing in heaven over one sinner who repents than over ninety-nine righteous persons who do not need to repent.

My dad drove me to my sister Julie's house. All the family was there. We cried together as we began to piece together what happened the night before Bobby took his life. Bobby and his girlfriend had recently had a son they had named Robert, Jr. One evening as we sat up together talking, Bobby shared his biggest fear with me. He said, "Tracie, I don't want to have kids because I am afraid that I will be a bad father like dad was, and I don't want to hurt my kids." The night Bobby died, my brother Paul was at Bobby's house. They talked for a bit, and Bobby was in a good mood. After Paul left, Bobby and his girlfriend had a fight. In anger, his girlfriend said, "you are a horrible father, and you are never going to see your child again." All of Bobby's innermost fears were triggered. He told her to come over but not to bring the baby. She never went, but when Bobby hung up the phone, he went into the garage. He stood on a red cooler and threw a cord over the beam in the garage. With a beer in his hand, all the emotion and hurt drove him to make a decision that could never be undone. The next morning a work friend stopped by to find the light on in the garage. He went in to find Bobby's lifeless body, and cut him down.

Bobby had so many friends who loved him. Each of them were heartbroken and forever affected by the decision he made. I don't blame anyone. You see, only Bobby could have made that decision that night. We all found ways to blame ourselves, and for a while I even blamed God. I know that Bobby's girlfriend would take back that night if she could. We all say things that we wish we could take back. I don't blame Bobby either. His brokenness caused him to lose hope. I wish he would have taken a walk, threw some dishes or even hit the wall that night. He didn't.

With all the details to tend to, we didn't have time to grieve. Bobby didn't have insurance, so we all split the arrangement costs. We ordered the suit, the casket, the flowers and the newspaper obituary. We answered all the calls and emails. We let everyone hug us. Being together helped as we drove together to complete the details. We found a preacher who agreed to do the service. I wondered how it would have been if he or someone like him had reached out to Bobby, what if they had encountered Bobby before the funeral, would the outcome have been different? It was the first funeral that we would plan, but unfortunately not the last. We made sure every detail was handled all the way down to the thank-you cards. Together, we struggled with knowing that little Robert would never know his father.

After the funeral, we cleaned out Bobby's house. His belongs were still there. The tools he used that night still sat in the garage. I can still see it as if it were that night. The broken beer bottle, the red cooler, the wire hanging from the rafter. What a horrible way to leave the earth. I remember wishing that I could have given him some of my grit. He would have looked death in the face and said, "Nice try, Sucker! I'm not letting you win!". Thankfully, I hold on to the fact that Death cannot hold him down. The resurrection power of Christ lives in him, and his spirit is very much alive!

John 16:13 (NIV) But when He, the Spirit of truth, comes, He will guide you into all the truth. He will not speak on His own; He will speak only what He hears, and he will tell you what is yet to come.

we got back to Tulsa, I went to a grief counseling class at church. My heart was so wounded. The class helped, but I wanted to be home with my family. The publishing company I worked for agreed to let me start working remotely, but my drive and focus were gone. Everything seemed pointless after Bobby was gone. I felt like God had betrayed me. I was doing everything I could to please him. I was sold out to Him, and now my brother was gone. There was nothing I could do. Everyone was looking at me for the answer to where Bobby was. In my heart, I feared the answer that I would have to share.

Suddenly, I remembered that God understood that there are those who can be sick in their minds. He knows their hurt. When I lined it up with the Word, I found agreement with that statement. Bobby had made a covenant with God. Even though he went off track, God honored His covenant because it was never based on Bobby's works. It was always based on God's love for him and His desire to restore relationship with all of His children. The Lord later gave me a dream, it was of Bobby in heaven having fun, and from that night, I had peace that we would all see Bobby again.

It took a while for me to bounce back. I found myself not wanting to go to church and not wanting to pursue God. Not exactly the picture perfect reaction, right? I should have said, God is in control and it will always work out for the best. But, it wasn't going to work out. Bobby wasn't coming back. Instead of pointing my anger at the Deceiver, I was mad at God. The Deceiver was the one who convinced Bobby that those lies about him were true. That enemy told Bobby that he wasn't good enough and that he would never be a good father. The devil is out to break us all. His desire is to destroy any potential that God has placed on the inside of us. He uses tragedy and trauma to do it.

John 10:10 (NIV) The thief comes only to steal and kill and destroy; I have come that they may have life, and have it to the full.

Even still, God pursued me. As I was driving with my windows rolled down and blasting the radio, smoking a cigarette in rebellion, I heard Him speak to me. "Tracie, is there anything I can do to make you love Me any less?" I replied, "No". He said, "Neither can you". That was it. Short and simple. He was giving me permission to hurt and even act out. We can walk out our journeys in our own style. I am glad He never told me to pick myself up or ask why I wasn't trusting Him. He let me move and breath in a style that is all my own. That is why I heard His voice that day. It was Love calling to me telling me that Love was waiting. Love wasn't rushing me. He wasn't angry. He was saying He would be there to pick up right where we left off when I was ready. He gave me the freedom to be angry and distant without the guilt. After that, I was ready to move forward with Him again.

If you have gone through a traumatic experience, get mad, act out if you need to. Just remember Satan is using that event to destroy your life. When you have to point your anger at someone, point it at the right source. Allow that anger to fuel a fire that says, "Satan, I have had enough of you stealing from me and my family! I am coming after you and your kingdom with a force you cannot contain! You will pay for every battle that you have brought across our path. You will pay for every life you have stolen!"

Chapter 6 Application: Tragedy hurts. There is just no getting around it. It leaves scars especially when someone you love leaves this earth. There is a part of you that is missing. Nothing can take away that pain at that moment. What you can do is keep moving forward. Find a new normal that allows for the pain. Satan will try to give you reasons to stop going to church or to isolate yourself. Don't let him win! He thinks that if he can keep you away from people, he can beat you so low that you will never get up again. Recognize that things will never be the same, and that is okay. The person that you lost wants you to keep moving forward and to find a place of peace and happiness again. They would not want you to stay broken and to give up. It is okay if you find yourself talking to the chair where they used to sit. It's okay to go to a gravesite and cry if that is what you need to heal your heart. But, don't stay mad at God.

God loves you and wants to hold you when you are lonely, upset and confused. God can provide a supernatural comfort that can't be described in words. When you are hurt, God hurts for you. When you cry, He sees every tear. His compassion for you runs deep, and He longs to take you to a place of refuge. There you can lean against Him, and He wraps His arms around you.

Rev: 21: 4 (BSB) God will wipe away every tear from our eyes. There will be no more death, neither sorrow, nor crying, neither shall there be any more pain for the former things are passed away.

Prayer: Heavenly Father, help us to forgive when it's hard to forgive. Help us to not judge people, but to see them the way that You see people with nothing missing and nothing broken walking out Your plans in their life. Heal the section of our hearts that belonged to those loved ones who are no longer with us. Help us to keep putting one foot in front of the other even when it doesn't seem to make any sense and when we don't know where we are going. Lead us to the place that begins and ends with You. Help us not to be callous in our dealings with others, but to be mindful that we all have families out there in need of a cheerleader. Help us to be the cheerleader for those suffering alone. Father, we thank You that you always deliver us to the other side of every trial and tragedy that would try to destroy us. You are a good, good Father who knows how to take care of His children. You pay attention to every detail in the plan you have for us. In Jesus Name, I pray. Amen.

CHAPTER 7

CANCER HR ER POSITIVE

I am going to be honest: Cancer sucks! Every part of it. From the first time you hear the word "cancer" to the moment you witness the damage it does to your loved one, it sucks! We have heard the word "cancer" our whole life, but when you hear you have it, you hear it in a new light and you hear it from a different perspective. For me, it became personal in multiple seasons in my life. It was different this time. I was not supporting a cause believing we need to find a cure for cancer. I was not reading an article saying this food or that food causes cancer. When the word is connected to someone that has touched your heart, it changes everything. When you see the tears and the heart break, you plead with everything you have. You search for a way to help stop the suffering of the one you love. When you hear that your beloved Grandmother has lung cancer or that your mom needs chemotherapy, everything changes. When you watch your close friends hold the hands of their child as they pass from this earth, everything changes.

When you look into the eyes of a loved one to tell them they have to fight, everything changes. It changes everyone and everything around them. It even changes some for the worse. Often people will look for someone to blame for their pain, their loss, their suffering. For them, the world is cold and heartless. They begin marking time until they can move beyond this life. They want to stop the pain that slowly destroys them. For others, they acknowledge their pain. They accept their loss and find a ray of sunshine in the clouds.

Those rays bring enough hope to keep them moving forward. God's love is brought to them through the love of family, friends and even strangers. They allow that love to strengthen them. They go on to live their lives in honor of the memory of those waiting on the other side.

Tragedy strikes everyone. Death is waiting at the doorsteps and will sweep in and take someone we love. Your heart will be shattered, and you will have to decide how to process the tragedy. What is the difference in those that find hope and those that only see pain? How do some people keep taking the hits but still move forward? Why do others become frozen in time? I can only speak from my experience on this. Having a strong relationship with the Lord will get you through the other side of the pain. God promised to never leave or forsake us, and He knows where all your broken pieces are. He knows exactly how to heal the deepest wounds.

On January 4, 2015, my hair salon was having a fundraiser. It was a cut-a-thon to benefit Bailey Bennett, an 8-year-old boy with brain cancer. The money raised from haircuts would go to Bailey and his family for treatments. Bailey was fighting brain cancer for the second time. He was first diagnosed in 2011 at the age of five. His mom and I instantly connected. She told me that Bailey wanted to give gifts to his nurses. He also wanted to put gifts into a prize box for siblings of cancer patients at Bronson Hospital. I just happened to have a trunk full of toys with me. Together we transferred all the toys to her car. Bailey was energetic and full of life. Because Bronson Hospital was one of my clients, I got the chance to see him and to drop off more toys to help keep the box full. It was a great blessing for me.

The next month, I was traveling a lot for work. I enjoyed meeting new people whom God would bring across my path on those trips. I was setting up my annual doctor's appointments to work around my schedule. I scheduled my mammogram as I would be turning 40 in a couple of months. When the time came, I walked into Paqui and Brian Kelly Comprehensive Breast Center to get my mammogram done. I was a little nervous not knowing what to expect so I decided I would share my journey on social media. It would be a reminder to all my friends to keep up with their annual exams. I went in for the test then let everyone know that it was no big deal. Then, I went back to my normal work routine.

February 12th, 2015 Social Media Post: 1st mammogram done! For the record, mammograms are painless and super easy!

Two days later, I received a call letting me know I needed to come back for a diagnostic mammogram. My sister Kim came into town and went with Eric and I. When we arrived, we went to the private office they led us to. We learned that they believed they saw cancer, but would like to do a needle core biopsy to confirm their suspicions. I don't remember how I reacted, but I tried to stay strong and not show how shaken I was inside.

Looking back, we should have stopped right there. We should have taken authority over the attack coming against my body. I'm not sure why we didn't. What I remember was being swept up in what was happening. Everything was moving so fast. We knew what to do, but we didn't do it. We knew the scriptures that said I was healed by His stripes, yet we never took authority.

Isaiah 53:5 (NIV) But He was pierced for our transgressions, He was crushed for our iniquities; the punishment that brought us peace was on Him, and by His wounds we are healed.

That is what we are called to do...ask the Lord for help. He is waiting to be invited into our situations. That has to be our first step. By doing so, we can avoid some of the roadblocks that will try to shut us down. It is an important step. He has already given us the scriptures to support that He is indeed on our side.

Matthew 8:1-3 (NKJV) When Jesus had come down from the mountain, great multitudes followed Him. And behold, a leper came and worshiped Him, saying, "Lord, if You are willing, You can make me clean." Then Jesus put out His hand and touched him, saying, "I am willing; be cleansed." Immediately his leprosy was cleansed.

Mark 11:24 (HCSB) Therefore I say unto you, What so ever you desire, when ye pray, believe that you receive [them], and you shall have [them].

Matthew 7:7 (HCSB) Ask, and it shall be given you; seek, and ye shall find; knock, and it shall be opened unto you:

John 14:13-14 (KJV) And whatsoever ye shall ask in my Name, that will I do, that the Father may be glorified in the Son.

Philippians 4:6-8 (KJV) Be careful for nothing; but in everything by prayer and supplication with thanksgiving let your requests be made known unto God.

John 15:7 (NIV) If you remain in me and my words remain in you, ask whatever you wish, and it will be done for you..

Matthew 21:22 (KJV) And all things, whatsoever ye shall ask in prayer, believing, ye shall receive.

Luke 18:1-8 (KJV) And he spoke a parable unto them [to this end], that men ought always to pray, and not to faint;

Luke 11:13 (NIV) If ye then, being evil, know how to give good gifts unto your children: how much more shall [your] heavenly Father give the Holy Spirit to them that ask him?

1 Kings 3:5 (NIV) At Gibeon the LORD appeared to Solomon during the night in a dream, and God said, "Ask for whatever you want me to give you."

John 16:24 (NIV) Until now you have not asked for anything in my name. Ask and you will receive, and your joy will be complete.

Psalms 37:4 (KJV) Delight thyself also in the LORD; and He shall give thee the desires of thine heart.

2 Corinthians 5:7(NIV) For we walk by faith, not by sight:

Matthew 7:7-12 (NIV) Ask and it will be given to you; seek and you will find; knock and the door will be opened to you. For everyone who asks receives; the one who seeks finds; and to the one who knocks, the door will be opened. Which of you, if your son asks for bread, will give him a stone? Or if he asks for a fish, will give him a snake? If you, then, though you are evil, know how to give good gifts to your children, how much more will your Father in heaven give good gifts to those who ask him! So in everything, do to others what you would have them do to you, for this sums up the Law and the Prophets.

There is no question what the Lord wants for your life! He is every ready to be your helper in every situation, He is simply waiting to be invited in.

Social Media Post: March 8th, 2015: People don't always need advice. Sometimes, all they really need is a hand to hold, an ear to listen, and a heart to understand them.

I got back from my trip to Wisconsin and had a follow-up appointment on the biopsy. I got the confirmation that it was breast cancer. I was told it was hormone and estrogen positive. That meant that the hormones in my body and those in the food I was eating were causing the cancer to grow at a faster rate.

March 10, 2015: The 1st results came in from the biopsy today. The results were that I have breast cancer, and I meet with the surgeon tomorrow. It is such a relief to know that we don't have to go through things alone, and that God is always with us making the crooked places straight. Isaiah 42:6 I will lead the blind by ways they have not known, along unfamiliar paths I will guide them; I will turn the darkness into light before them and make the rough places smooth. These are the things I will do; and I will not forsake them.

March 10, 2015: You've only got three choices in life: Give up, give in or give it all you've got.

March 11th, 2015

I had a question as to why I have chosen to share my experience on social media. Honestly, my initial feeling on the matter was that I was going to get my first baseline mammogram and wanted to show that it was no big deal and encourage others to be proactive in their healthcare as well. As it progressed I wanted others to realize that even strong women of God, who know God as their companion, guardian, friend, and healer have curve balls thrown at them. Then, it became that I needed to let people know that just because they have something happen to them, it doesn't mean that God doesn't love, care, protect, and heal them. I received a lot of feedback wondering how I am, where I am in my faith, what I am believing for etc. So here is my answer, God loves me so much that he took a girl who grew up in a pretty bad situation, who quit school as a freshman, and got pregnant before I was married. He took that girl who had no clear moral guidelines and turned her into someone that will not waiver at the promises of God regardless of what comes her way. He turned me into someone that when I tell my story people don't believe it because they can't recognize that part of my life anymore. So if you think the doctors saying that I have cancer, or that them may need to remove a part of my body is going to make me waiver you are mistaken. This girl doesn't quit, she doesn't give up, and she has a huge God who always has her back.

If all that was left of me was a thankful heart when I get to heaven, me and that thankful heart are going to meet Jesus and thank him for the transformation that he has done in my life and for all of His faithful promises that were constantly fulfilled in my life. Anyone can be average, anyone can listen to the devils lies, and quit and give up, lie around feeling sorry for yourself, but I don't have time for that.   I was created for a purpose and I plan to keep fulfilling that purpose until the day that I meet my heavenly Father.

March 12th, 2015

I left to go out of town for a work trip to Wisconsin. I wanted a little space from everyone and room to express myself without worrying about being strong just for a minute. The drive was exactly what I needed, I was able to process what was happening, and I had to wait for more results to come back so it was a great way to distract myself. That trip I went to Green Bay to meet with the Green Bay Packers and Bellin Health System to discuss mobile display advertising. In the back of mind, thoughts were coming a mile a minute on what would come back and how we would address the obstacles ahead.

March 12th, 2015

Lunchtime struggles: With everything going on I forgot to pack a few things for my business trip. I stopped by Kohls to grab a couple of things over lunch. Apparently the undergarment section now causes me a little anxiety. After evaluating what was going on, I realized it's because my body will be undergoing some pretty extreme changes that were not by my choice. I find myself tempted to wonder how my husband will react to the changes etc. It is an unreasonable fear, after all he thought I was beautiful before I had braces, while I was pregnant with four children, while I was 100 pounds overweight, and when everything started sagging after my weight loss. It got me thinking how we place so much importance on what others think, and how we try to figure out what people think about us, often imagining the worst. So today rest in the fact that God loves you just the way that you are and thinks you are very valuable!

Matthew 10:29-31 (NIV) Are not two sparrows sold for a penny? And not one of them will fall to the ground apart from your Father. But even the hairs of your head are all numbered. Fear not, therefore; you are of more value than many sparrows.

March 29, 2015 at 10:15pm

So this was the most difficult weekend so far in this Cancer Journey. I happened upon a fabulous google image of what a double mastectomy scar with lymph node removal looks like. I then decided to not address how I was feeling and just allow it to let me be short with my family. I went on a 5 mile walk so that I could feel sorry for myself. I forced myself to go to church, and there were a thousand distractions, but I am thankful for a woman who knows how to be led by the spirit, and kept the atmosphere where it needed to be so that I could hear from God. You see this journey we take is not easy and The devil is tricky, he wants to defeat you in any way that he can. But God fights for you, and you win! Stay strong

Tammy Cook-Laskowski Sending you prayers and hugs. You are one strong woman! Thank you for sharing your journey. You are inspirational and will whoop cancers butt!

March 29, 2015

Jane Bryant Harbin Tracie, don't forget about my offer. I have been down the road you are going down and I got the victory with God.. You will to. Email, message, or call me. I will continue praying for you. It is not easy, but it will save your life. That is the way you kick the devil in the face. You are very much on the right road by facing the facts and letting go and let your frustrations come out. . God will see you through this but there will be bad days and you will come through those and come out of them and kick the devil again in the face.

March 29, 2015

Lisa Duke Love you. Allow yourself to be human, to feel anger and self-pity. Its ok! Just don't stay there. Its ok.

March 29, 2015

Anu Roosaare Barger Tracie, I've been through the exact procedure and have learned to love myself again. It wasn't easy, so I know what you're going through. Actually, just today I had a thought that I will never have to worry about saggy boobs! Message me if you want to talk. I'm praying for you.

March 29, 2015

Patrick McNamara Prayers and never feel sorry for yourself please we are all here as support

March 29, 2015

Bob Carter This Test will become your Testimony. Standing in faith and agreement with you.

March 29, 2015

Mellony Fisher Clark love you Tracie ~ stay strong and don't let this stop your passion. There's endless things to accomplish and you're needed for the job! Praying for You

March 29, 2015

Gwen-Ann Redfearn Tracie, while I didn't have a double, definitely had lymph nodes removed as well, wasn't able to have reconstruction done for a few years, yet the 'pityest' day was the day shaved my head.. Again, that's the day a woman of Grace shared her journey. God will continue to bless you as you go! I admire you for admitting your weakness even as you celebrate the strengths.

March 29, 2015

Maureen Cleveland The outward appearance of your body cannot change the inward beauty of your soul. Know that your 'feelings' are human, but your victory is heavenly! Find someone who you can feel safe to spill those feelings out to yet will give you the encouragement, agreement, scripture to stand on, and lots of hugs!

March 29, 2015

Carol Holley I love you Tracie! It's ok to have bad days! You & God will conquer this! I'm praying for you!

March 29, 2015

Don Glassburn Just remember all of us are praying for you and God is soo good.

March 30, 2015

Linda Chrisman I am praying for you and your family and it is ok to have bad days God is always with you and you will win this battle with Gods help

March 30, 2015 *Patti Welton Ries Praying*

March 30, 2015

Dorothy Fretz Satan is so aware of our vulnerabilities and weak areas, whether physical, spiritual or emotional. Remember he's that roaring lion always ready for an attack and his crafty schemes appear in so many ways. You are being covered through scores of prayers and may you sense the nearness of God surrounding you with His peace, love and comfort. "May those chains that seem to bind you, fall helplessly behind you when you praise Him!" This old Russ Taff song came to mind as I read your account.

March 30, 2015

Terrinna Thybault You said it perfectly.!!! Again thanks for being transparent.. love u and praying for u and u family.xo

March 30, 2015

Barbara Brooks Harvey I think you are allowed an occasional pity party as long as you don't stay there! My mom always told me that God never gives you anything that you and he together can't handle and I have found that to be true..

you will too. I will continue to keep you in my prayers.

March 30, 2015

Jeanette Marie Tracie thanks for posting this. It's such an up and down experience. Continue to post so we know you need some extra grace on the journey. I'm praying today for What is in your highest good to be present to you today. Much love!

March 30, 2015

Barbara Perry Will continue to lift you up in prayer Tracie !

March 30, 2015

Winston Watson May grace and peace be with you. "Now thanks be unto God, which always causeth us to triumph in Christ, and maketh manifest the savour of his knowledge by us in every place." 2 Corinthians 2:14

March 30, 2015

Patty Wheeler You are an amazing child of a God and he is going to use this journey to allow you to bring non-believers to him, you will save lives, I know that I was behind on scheduling my "pancake test" and scheduled and had mine last week, pushed my sister n law and she has scheduled hers. So continue with your strength in God. If you ever need a friend to pray with I am a phone call away. Continued prayers and love in Christ for you!

March 30, 2015 *Kenia Salazar Sawyer You are loved and thought of more than you know ms. Tracie Beck Hunsberger. You are prayed for with much, much love. My dearest godmother who is now in her late 70's went through the same procedure many years ago. But it is a time we will not forget. You remind me much of her. Her tough cookie yet sensitive and sweet attitude. She lives in Mexico and I got to see her a few weeks ago. Once again showed me her scar and*

the smile of courage that she displays. She walks 7 miles every other day to my 94 year old grandmother home and visits with her. Rain or shine she is there. You are one of them. A woman of great courage.

March 30, 2015

Kenia Salazar Sawyer By the way she wears her scars as if it were a battle medallion of some kind. Together with her heart surgery scars. And yet somehow I don't know how she is able to look back and laugh at tough moments and speak with much compassion and kindness towards those who are now in difficult situations.

March 30, 2015

Patricia Penrose im ss my baby sister is going through this but god will give u strength to get through it and your an inspiration to many i went to doc last wk and they are supposed to be scheduling my mamogram if you need me i can come over or meet you somewhere love you unconditionally and you wil pull thourgh this your a stong woman of God

March 30, 2015

Dawn Kozsey You are so wise and transparent that you are a blessing and witness to all who know you. Life is a struggle, and the devil, our accuser. May God bless you daily and may His presence be your strong guide always. Thank you for the wisdom you share that touches our hearts, especially mine.

April 2nd 2015 was the day a piece of me was removed. It was the day of the double mastectomy with reconstruction surgery to remove the cancer. It was twelve days before my 40th birthday. My whole family came with me the day of the surgery each wearing a specially designed t-shirt that were given to them by my coworkers. The shirts said, "Faith Love Cure Tracie". We all tried to keep the mood light. I applied skin care on all of my sisters as we waited. I invent work in my life when I need to deal with issues that I am not ready to face. I wasn't scared, but I was aware of the tough road I had ahead. Eric was there holding my hand knowing the fear behind my smile. He prayed over me before I went under. I went to sleep knowing I would wake safely afterwards.

My hospital stay lasted for two days. I went home patched together physically but was unable to process everything that just happened. Family, friends, co-workers and complete strangers stood by me. They brought meals, gift cards and words of encouragement. Whatever the need, someone offered to help. At one point, I was desperate to shower and wash my hair. My salon offered to wash my hair. I can't tell you what a blessing that was! I felt like a woman again. God pays attention to all those details. He knew that was important to me so He made sure someone was there to meet that need. Something was happening to me on the inside as well. I began to lose the selfish part of myself. As I saw others around me stepping up for us, I realized that life is about taking care of people. Even the most independent people will at some point need the care of others. I could rest knowing there were capable, gifted people stepping up for us.

As I healed, Eric slept on the couch next to me. He took care of the four drainage tubes I had. He told me that I was beautiful. The girls cleaned and made dinner. When one of the girls got sick, Alyssa cleaned up and did the laundry. It all got done. I let them take care of me, I let the girls take care of each other, and together we made it through. We all had scars. I did, Eric did and the kids did. However, we all got back up. We put one foot in front of the other. We survived all the surgeries, the doctor appointments and even the momentary shaking of our faith. It's what we do. We get back up. We face fear, and we say we cannot be defeated.

On the more difficult days, I tried to do something for someone else. I took toys to the hospital. I filled up random people's gas tanks. I gave money to the barista at Starbucks asking her to keep paying for coffee until the money ran out. I would also sit and have real conversations with the people in my neighborhood. I got to know an elderly woman better while helping her pick up limbs in her yard. I shared a good book with her and asked her advice on raising teenagers. I did whatever I could to take the focus off myself. I put that energy into serving others, and it was then that I began to get better.

As I got better, I felt the need to take on new challenges.

In fact, on October 25 2016 I was featured on the Bowflex insider

Team Tracie's Story: Redefining Yourself through Fitness

Posted On Oct 25, 2016 By Bowflex Insider Team

Tracie Hunsberger, 41, had always been independent and on the go. As a national digital sales manager, the mother of four travelled frequently for work and had a regular fitness routine — until her world was turned upside down.

In February 2015, the South Bend, Indiana, native was diagnosed with breast cancer and elected to undergo a double mastectomy. Her surgery left her with no strength in her arms and feeling dependent on others and on her faith on God.

In addition, every time Tracie started making progress toward regaining her strength, she found herself having to undergo another surgery.

"Working out after my surgeries was really challenging for me because I couldn't do a lot of extreme motions. Even lifting any amount of weight was hard," Tracie recalled. "I couldn't even get a cup out of the cupboard. I had trouble getting my suitcase in and out of the car or going through airports. All of those things that were second nature to who I was were taken away."

Tired of feeling vulnerable, Tracie knew she needed to commit to rebuilding her strength. After trying a variety of workouts, she found she needed something that would offer fluid motion and be gentler on her joints. Her solution? The Bowflex Max Trainer®.

"The 14-minute workout is a big draw for me. Who couldn't do something for 14 minutes?" Tracie said. "I found a workout that was gentle enough to allow me to get started and yet challenged me to push further each time — building strength and increasing the flexibility in my arms."

With the help of fitness and her trust in God, Tracie was able to gradually loosen the muscles that had limited her post-surgeries and achieved her goal of getting stronger. Today, she is feeling healthier than ever.

"A lot of healing, recovery is attitude and perception," Tracie explained. "A situation is as bad as you think it is. Fitness allowed me to make a mental shift. I wasn't identified by cancer anymore."

What advice does Tracie have for others who are just starting their fitness journeys?

"Working out is like anything," Tracie said. "The first few times are going to stretch you, and it's going to be difficult. But every time you do it, you'll get a little stronger and you'll breathe a little easier. It's a lot more fun."

Chapter 7 Application: When you find yourself a little more vulnerable than you would like, remember that you are part of a community. You don't have to do it alone. It's okay to share your feelings. Let others help you when you feel your most vulnerable. That is what we are here for. Your family, friends and even strangers want to be there for you when you come out on the other side. They want to rejoice with you along the way. Because of your friends and family, you are never alone on your journey.

Deuteronomy 31:8 (NIV) The LORD himself goes before you and will be with you; He will never leave you nor forsake you. Do not be afraid; do not be discouraged.

Joshua 1:5 (NIV) No one will be able to stand up against you all the days of your life. "As I was with Moses, so I will be with you; I will never leave you nor forsake you."

1 Kings 8:57 (NKJV) May the LORD our God be with us as he was with our fathers; may He never leave us nor forsake us.

1 Chronicles 28:20 (NIV) David also said to Solomon his son, "Be strong and courageous, and do the work. Do not be afraid or discouraged, for the LORD God, my God, is with you. He will not fail you or forsake you until all the work for the service of the temple of the LORD is finished."

Psalms 37:28 (NIV) For the LORD loves the just and will not forsake his faithful ones. They will be protected forever, but the offspring of the wicked will be cut off.

Psalms 94:14 (NIV) For the LORD will not reject his people; He will never forsake His inheritance.

Isaiah 41:17 (NIV) The poor and needy search for water, but there is none;

their tongues are parched with thirst. But I the LORD will answer them; I, the God of Israel, will not forsake them.

Isaiah 42:16 (NIV) I will lead the blind by ways they have not known, along unfamiliar paths I will guide them; I will turn the darkness into light before them and make the rough places smooth. These are the things I will do; I will not forsake them.

Hebrews 13:5 (NIV) Keep your lives free from the love of money and be content with what you have, because God has said, "Never will I leave you; never will I forsake you."

We may leave God, but He will never leave us. No matter how bleak the situation, no matter how empty the feeling comes, God will never leave you! His promises are true. His word is above all! We can move forward because, He goes before us. And if God be for us, who can be against us?

There is none like Him, and He will not allow His word to return to Him void!

Isaiah 55:11 (NIV) So will My Word be which goes forth from My mouth; It will not return to Me empty, Without accomplishing what I desire, And without succeeding in the matter for which I sent it.

Prayer: Heavenly Father, I lift up those who are going through challenging times. Times when we find ourselves questioning your character and your love for us. Thank you that during those times, we don't have to qualify for your help or the help of others. It is not about our perfection, knowledge or strength, but simply your love for us. You love us so much that you sent your only Son to die on the cross so that our fellowship with you could be restored. You will never stop working on our behalf. I thank you that you are moving now by reminding us that every word of the Bible is true. What it says we can have, we can have. Help us to find the strength to invite you into our situations allowing you to work in our weakness. Let us realize there is nothing we can do to make You love us any less or any more than you already do. Your love is not about us being good enough, working hard enough or being beautiful enough. It has always been about you desiring us and pursuing us. Your love exceeds anything we could ever comprehend. You will always be there waiting for us to invite you into our situations. We thank You for that. We thank You for pursuing us and never leaving us. Thank you for the friends you send along the way to encourage and help us. Give us the wisdom to be an encourager for someone else. In Jesus Name we pray. Amen.

CHAPTER 8

MY LOVE STORY

I hope this book has strengthened your faith in God. I hope that in this story you saw a girl who by her own means could do nothing. It was only as she trusted in God and allowed Him to guide her steps from one to the next. All she had to do was keep moving forward.

Eric and I serve in ministry by traveling to churches to share our story of God's faithfulness to us. He has called me to tell you not to give up. When you find yourself hurt and all you can think to do is stop in your tracks, realize that God wants to take you to new levels.

He wants to show you things that you can only do with His help. It takes trust and a willingness to be vulnerable.

Along the way, I have experienced hurt both inside of and outside of the church, by family and during my career. However, I did not give up on the church, my family, and I didn't stop working. Satan will use all sorts of tactics to try to get you off your course. The easiest tactic is for him to work through people. Refuse to walk away from the support in your life because you are going through something tough. During tough times, remember God loves you. He will never leave you, and He will see you through to the other side. His Word is true. He will do what the Bible say He will do. Don't allow your flesh to get in the way and slow down the process. He wants to heal every part of you. All you have to do is trust Him by giving Him your situation and allowing Him to work it out.

I have often tried to figure out God. Surely, He didn't know everything that needed to happen, so I would offer to help Him out. Let me do this or that to make sure things will work out in my favor. The problem with doing things in my own ability is that the minute I brought it out of the spiritual realm, I had to make it happen in the natural. That required my own strength, knowledge and ability. You can see from this story how flawed I am. There was no way that I could have done what God did for me. He took a Subway employee making $3.35 an hour into a life that she could never have made happen on her own. He provided connections, education, supernatural wisdom and favor for me exactly when I needed it. Let God work on your behalf. He knows the beginning from the end. He knows the dreams He has placed inside of you. He knows every situation and event that has to happen for things to work out in your favor.

I had to step off into deep water when I wasn't sure if I knew how to swim. I sold homes I loved, I moved to new states, I trusted God for finances and jobs. Every time I made a choice to trust Him. Each time I operated in obedience even when it made no logical sense. I came out stronger every day.

God is not a respecter of people, He took me from the projects to one of the nicest homes in our neighborhood. He can do that for you too. It all starts with a relationship. Get to know His heart for you. He loves you when you have nothing to give, when you do nothing and when you look like nothing to the outside world. It is because He created you and planted seeds inside of you, that you were meant to bloom.

The world will do everything to bury the seed. It will try to convince you that you are not strong enough, pretty enough, smart enough, good enough or even rich enough. But, what they don't know is that you have the X Factor...a secret weapon that works on your behalf. Mixing that unique seed with the Father's love stirs up a potential that the world has never seen, cannot comprehend and cannot stop!

You are created with a divine purpose that makes you special. There is a plan for you that only you can do. You can slow it down or even stop it if you chose. Your success or failure is not contingent on any external situation or event. Your success is dependent on your ability to trust God in every situation. Allow Him to show Himself faithful and watch Him perform His Word in your life.

We will never understand what life will bring, especially the spiritual part of it. Because we are the creation, we will never fully understand our Creator. What we can know is God's heart. It is when we know His heart that we know His love for us, for our families and our communities. In times of difficulties, He is moved with compassion. He will pursue us. If we feel incapable, we can remember *Philippians 4:13 "I can do all things through Christ Who strengthens me. That spiritual law supersedes anything that is going on in the natural. If you receive a bad report from a doctor, remember Isaiah 53:5, "He was pierced for our transgressions, He was crushed for our iniquities; the punishment that brought us peace was upon Him, and by His wounds we are healed."*

Spiritual laws always triumph over natural laws. If you get a report or someone tells you something and the Word of God tells you something different, stay with the Word of God. Spiritual laws always triumph over natural laws! If God says you are healed and the doctor's report says you are sick, stay with the Word. If you bank account says you are broke, remember the Word of God says all of your needs are met.

Stay with the Word. If you feel worthless, alone, and afraid of the future, and the Word says that you are valuable and that God has a PLAN just for you, stick with the Word. I promise if you hold onto the Word and walk in God's love, you will see the spiritual laws working on your behalf. Don't give up, God is waiting to show Himself faithful to you.

Faith in God's ability and not our own is true faith. My husband always says, **"Faith doesn't even start until it's impossible for us to do it on our own."** So, if you are facing the impossible, know that you CAN do all things through Christ who strengthens you!

When you are up against an impossible situation, know *that God has a promise for you!*

Proverbs 3:5-6 (NIV) Trust in the LORD with all your heart and lean not on your own understanding; in all your ways submit to him, and he will make your paths straight.

Philippians 4:13 says that "You can do ALL things THROUGH Christ who strengthens you!"

Luke 1:37 (NIV) For no word from God will ever fail.

Mark 11:22 (NIV) "Have faith in God," Jesus answered.

John 15:7 (NIV) If you remain in Me and My Words remain in you, ask whatever you wish, and it will be done for you. Luke 18:27 (NIV) Jesus replied, "What is impossible with man is possible with God."

CHAPTER 9

CHOICES

Today make the choice to sell out to the plan of God for your life. Choose to even go out into the deep water with Him if He calls you there. I promise that you will come out Stronger Every Day.

Jesus wants to be the Lord of your life. That means He wants you to trust Him and allow Him to lead you in your choices and decisions. He also wants to be your Savior meaning He wants to save you from the consequences of your sin. That is what He did for you when He died on the cross. He took your sins upon Himself. If you don't know Him as your personal Lord and Savior, I would like to pray with you. All God asks is for you to come to Him with a sincere heart and accept His plan of salvation through His Son, Jesus Christ. The Bible says in Romans 10:9 that *"if you believe on the Lord Jesus Christ with your heart and confess it with your mouth, you will be saved."* Your sins will be washed away when you accept what Jesus did for you.

Simply pray:

Lord Jesus, come into my life. Forgive me of all my sins. I believe that You are the Son of God and that You died on the cross for me. You rose from the dead to make a way for me. Thank You for loving me enough to die for me and for thinking that I was worth it.

Today, I accept You into my heart and give myself one hundred percent to you. I am tired of living my own way in my own strength and ability. I want to live Your plan and purpose. I need Your help. Create in me a clean heart and guide my journey from this day forward. I will follow You wherever You take me.

I will trust You as my Lord and Savior. I love you, Jesus, and I accept you as my Savior. You are now Lord over my life, and I trust You to get me through to the other side, stronger every day.

If you prayed this prayer, Congratulations! You are starting a new life with a clean slate. No one can take that away from you.

Write to us. Let us know how we can pray for you. Share your testimonies with us, so that we can rejoice in your victories. If you prayed the above prayer, let us know about your decision to follow Christ. We will stand in agreement with you as you start your new journey and become STRONGER EVERYDAY!

WE LOVE YOU AND PRAY GOD'S BLESSING OVER YOU AND YOUR FAMILY!.

Eric and Tracie Hunsberger

Romans831 Ministries

The End

ABOUT THE AUTHOR

As an Author, Speaker, and Sales and Marketing Leader Tracie Hunsberger uses wisdom gained in the trenches of life to speak to the deep questions of faith that individuals often want to ask but are afraid to say. Connect with Tracie www.traciehunsberger.com

Write to Tracie and share your story

Together we are changing the World

Tracie Hunsberger

18811 East 42nd Street

Tulsa, OK 74134

Romans 8:31

What, then, shall we say in response to these things? If God is for us, who can be against us?

Made in the USA
Columbia, SC
05 August 2017